D1709700

DEDICATION

The Bolender Center would not be here today without the uncompromising dedication and unwavering perseverance of a number of people. Chief among them are Julia Irene Kauffman and Jeff Bentley. Julia, for providing the vision and resources to keep the idea alive and insuring that it became a reality. And Jeff, for maintaining a personal focus and commitment to the mission that kept the board, patrons, various committees and the entire design and construction team aligned to insure that the Ballet had a home that was not just any home but one of the best dance facilities in the world.

BNIM

POWER

REVIVING A HISTORIC BUILDING
THE TODD BOLENDER CENTER FOR DANCE & CREATIVITY

STEPHEN MCDOWELL
INTRODUCTION BY MARLON BLACKWELL

ORO
EDITIONS

CONTENTS

FOREWORD

Michael M. Kaiser

"IT IS TRULY AN EXCELLENT DANCE BUILDING. I'M LUCKY ENOUGH TO TRAVEL ALL OVER THE WORLD AND SEE DANCE FACILITIES EVERYWHERE AND I CAN'T THINK OF ONE IN THE WORLD THAT IS MORE BEAUTIFUL THAN THIS BUILDING."

2011 Grand Opening of the Todd Bolender Center for Dance & Creativity

───────

It was a great honor for me to be invited to speak at the opening of the Todd Bolender Center in October 2011. My arts management career started in 1985 in Kansas City with the Kansas City Ballet. I had virtually no relevant arts management experience and literally no knowledge of ballet. But the board—and Todd (Bolender)—were willing to take a risk on me and I learned more about arts management and dance than I could have imagined.

Todd did not just teach me about steps and turn out and choreography. He also taught me about striving for excellence; he would accept nothing less. I learned about the vibrancy of the arts scene in Kansas City, a vitality that has continued to grow and develop since I left in 1987.

In fact, Kansas City is investing in the arts at a time when so many other cities and towns are reducing their interest in and support for the arts. The opening of the Bolender Center celebrates the remarkable role the arts play in this city.

The development of new technology has given our potential audience members new forms of entertainment and new ways to spend their discretionary time and money, making it far more difficult to sell tickets at prices that cover some, if not all, of the cost of production.

This is happening, of course, at a time of great financial instability. Expensive projects and productions seem death defying rather than simply scary. But risk taking is necessary to attract new audiences.

And our audiences—young people, many of whom have had virtually no arts education—have little or no exposure to the arts at all. If we do not invest in the arts education of our children, who will be our future audience, board members, donors and volunteers of the future?

A recent study on arts education in the United States commissioned by the President's Committee on the Arts and the Humanities included this chilling statistic: "Among children of a college graduates, 27% said they had never taken a single arts class, compared with 12% in 1982. For children of high-school graduates, the number who'd never had any arts study rose from 30% nearly 30 years ago to 66% in 2008."

This radical diminution in exposure of children to arts education has dire consequences for our arts ecology as well as our nation as a whole.

Despite all of these challenges, I remain an optimist. These problems are daunting but solvable. And Kansas City seems perfectly situated to play a major role in leading the way.

The openings of the Todd Bolender Center for Dance & Creativity and the Kauffman Center for the Performing Arts mark Kansas City as an unusual outlier: a city with the desire to invest more in the arts rather than less.

I have great hope that those same donors who have been so generous in building these structures are going to value the work created within these structures. I trust that the wonderful arts organizations here will develop work that attracts new audiences and donors. I have hope that Kansas City's theaters, museums, dance companies, symphony and chamber music ensembles can thrive and grow the important, surprising art that attracts local and national audiences and donors.

If so, Kansas City can continue to be renowned for its cultural life and the way the arts are ingrained in the life of the community. Clearly, no one arts organization can accomplish this goal alone.

Kansas City can continue to live up to its potential by embracing a plan for its cultural life that ensures: every child has a systematic arts education; arts organizations work together to develop arts projects of size and scope that attract national and international attention; diverse cultural opportunities are offered to a broad spectrum of the population; ticket prices are affordable to the entire community and that training for artists is available and that Kansas City becomes a home for artists, not simply a place for them to visit.

Moreover, it is vital that these great new facilities are put to maximum use. There are so many ways that the Bolender Center can benefit the cultural life of this community.

I can see a future where a strong image for Kansas City arts is viewed across the nation. Kansas City has had robust arts organizations for decades, but with few exceptions, they are not well enough known around the nation.

When we brought the Kansas City Ballet to the Kennedy Center as part of our "Ballet Across America" program, the company was a favorite of audiences and critics alike. The company was also a surprise to many. This should not be. And I see a future where it will not be.

Kansas City is poised to become a true national leader. I do not see many other cities with the same opportunity to take the lead; in fact, in this difficult economic climate, most cities are going in reverse and losing their arts organizations, artists and reputations.

There are great benefits available to cities acknowledged to be great arts cities: increases in national funding, tourism and access to the best artists to name just three. And when more money, both earned and contributed, flows into an arts ecology it can create bigger, better, more surprising art, and larger audiences and donor bases that support even more growth and financial stability. The payoff can be huge.

It would especially gratifying to me that the opening of the Bolender Center would be one important catalyst in achieving this scenario.

Todd, I know, would be especially pleased. He was a man with great taste and high standards. He would have loved this building, but what he would have loved more was that it was erected because the Kansas City community so valued this company.

THE SUPPORTING LEG

Marlon Blackwell, FAIA and David Buege

The pleasures of architecture and the pleasures of dance are immediate and visceral, intellectual as well as sensual. Each has a classical aspect and many of their most fundamental principles persist, surviving the vicissitudes. Each has an essential lexicon as well and, if we make the effort to know them, these make things more accessible and therefore more rewarding. Meaning, for which postmodern architects were in hot pursuit, was often superficial and not so satisfying as it was intended to be. Certain principles provide an armature for those new ones that emerge in response to new technologies, to economic ambitions and cultural change, to crisis and constraints. Ideas can be transitory and contingent on changes in fashion, often they might seem lost in jargon, opaque, obscure and of questionable significance. Today it is sometimes difficult to distinguish the names of architectural offices from those of rock-and-roll bands, not necessarily a bad thing, but in contemporary practice architecture too commonly suffers from excess and diminishment by the ravages of novelty.

Architecture is arguably a fairly simple thing, an elemental thing of windows and doors, walls and roofs, definitive and necessary things that are the raw material of architecture and that demand architects' close attention. All of these may be subjected to processes of complication, transformation or exaggeration. Sometimes it is better to simplify, to exercise restraint. In the best, most deeply affecting architecture, there may be complication and restraint that has been carefully balanced. This is certainly true for BNIM's interventions in Jarvis Hunt's Power House.

Le Corbusier once suggested that we find "architecture" where a window is too large or too small, but merely a "building" when windows are the correct or conventional size. Perhaps we shouldn't take this too literally. It may best be understood as an admonition to question convention and to consider even the most prosaic things with great care. Hunt's Power House had great windows and these remain, having been carefully restored. BNIM has made them greater with the shading devices for south-facing windows (p. 101). Easily overlooked, they are beautiful as well as useful in their own quiet way, as machines.

Arguments about the primacy of space or form, form or function, can be like arguments over the relative virtues of the Beatles and the Rolling Stones. Ludwig Mies van der Rohe described architecture as the will of an epoch translated into space, an opera Wagner unfortunately never got around to writing. In much of Mies' own work this was exemplified in the careful use of materials and the exacting resolution of detail, often in support of universal space configured with great restraint, especially late in his career. Better to be good than interesting, Mies said, and this could be said of Hunt's Power House, too. While not a monument, it was built to a high standard, solid and substantial, dignified and circumspect. Planned obsolescence hadn't yet been invented, and the idea of a limited lifespan for a building was perhaps not so prevalent as now. A significantly different subsequent use was probably not an important consideration for most buildings. The space of the Power House was designed to accommodate great machines, not to conform to their shapes. The Bolender Center now illustrates the great virtue in this.

WHEN THE ARTIST RISES HIGH ENOUGH TO ACHIEVE THE BEAUTIFUL, THE SYMBOL BY WHICH HE MAKES IT PERCEPTIBLE TO MORTAL SENSES BECOMES OF LITTLE VALUE IN HIS EYES, WHILE HIS SPIRIT POSSESSES ITSELF IN THE ENJOYMENT OF THE REALITY.
Nathaniel Hawthorne

Hunt kept his office in Chicago's Monadnock Building, still considered by some to be that city's single finest piece of architecture more than a hundred years after its construction. Hunt's decision to situate his architectural practice there was likely not a simple matter of available space. At sixteen habitable stories, the Monadnock's perimeter brick-bearing walls, six feet thick at their base, were at the effective limit of this type of skyscraper construction. At the client's insistence, the architecture of the Monadnock was without ornament, spare and refined. Hunt's own Butler Brothers warehouse in Jersey City is a powerful illustration of a building of similar character and these same qualities. The Power House represents these qualities and the same sensibility, more quietly in a smaller building.

Hunt's Chicago contemporaries included Louis Sullivan, seven years older, and Daniel Burnham and Edward Bennett, who were responsible for the 1909 Plan of Chicago. With the exception of Sullivan, who had been dismissive of Burnham's Columbian Exposition of 1893, all were advocates for the principles of the *City Beautiful* movement. Hunt's Union Station is Kansas City's most emblematic *City Beautiful* monument, and only a suggestion of what Kansas City and other cities might have been had the vision been more fully realized. The *City Beautiful* was singular and idealized as a vision for the design of cities, at odds with the pragmatic, loosely planned American industrial city of which the Power House is a bit more representative.

The Power House is exceedingly modest in contrast to Union Station, as one might expect such a building to be, and not at all unusual for its time. Comparisons of Hunt's Power House with the "Jewel Box banks" of Louis Sullivan, late-career works of similar decorum that are scattered across several Midwest states and that followed the construction of the Power House closely in time, might not be too far fetched. The Power House, like the banks, is simple in form and orthogonal. Sullivan's banks are distinguished by the quality and exuberance of their ornament. Only modest decorative touches were applied to the Power House,

mostly related to the large windows to enhance or exaggerate their perceived size. The Power House is a generic building in the best sense. How many buildings built today to serve a similar purpose to that of the Power House will be so readily adapted to new purposes in their future?

Architecture is in countless ways a different thing now than it was when Hunt built Union Station and the Power House. Modern architecture appeared in the interim and achieved preeminence for its inherent economies more than its social program, only to suffer from a loss of faith on the part of architects and indifference, or worse, in the general population. Architects for a time returned with a vengeance to architecture's historical past for meaning, for legitimacy and to reestablish the popular accessibility lost, it was argued, to the characteristic flatness that Frank Lloyd Wright identified in modern architecture. BNIM's remarkable portfolio demonstrates that modern architecture can still be great when free of dogma and not doctrinaire, but especially when architects make the most of their opportunities with as much conviction as intelligence.

The metaphor of the palimpsest gained currency in the discourse of postmodern architecture, referring literally to the erasure by scraping of the surface of parchment made from animal skins, common practice in the Middle Ages. The durable surface of parchment was prepared to receive a new text and this process could be repeated, again and again. Especially in documents from the earliest centuries of the Middle Ages, before the use of pumice was introduced to erase more thoroughly, traces and layers of older texts remained faintly legible. This metaphor was used by architects to suggest that cities could be built in similar ways, layer upon layer, to create a more complex city fabric. Buildings like the Power House and the new architecture of the Bolender Center, built within and layered upon, suggest this metaphor as well. There are economic and ecological virtues in the renovation and adaptive reuse of buildings, and the possibility for placing one such text upon another allows for a new use with new or additional meanings when layered in this way.

Giovanni Battista Piranesi, *The Round Tower, plate III from Invenzioni Capric di Carceri*, between 1747 and 1751

The *carceri d'invenzione* of Giovanni Battista Piranesi, the space of imaginary prisons rendered in the mid-eighteenth century as a series of prints, informed neoclassicism. They may have anticipated the complexity and dynamics of interior spaces for machinery and industrial operations centuries later, and have parallels in the work of Charles Scheeler and Charles Demuth, twentieth-century artists who saw the compositional power of industrial stacks like that of the Power House and the formal qualities like those in the hoppers that have been preserved, in painterly fashion in orange, in the Bolender Center. Piranesi drew sixteen views in his *carceri* series. There are several photographs in this book that provide views of strikingly similar spaces with dense assemblages of equivalent modern elements of architecture, lacking the horrific aspect of the *carceri* but with a powerful

affective presence nevertheless. When first installed the power-generating equipment of the Power House was probably painted black or battleship gray (or some other industrial equivalent), beautiful in an industrial aesthetic sort of way but certainly nothing so chromatic as in the Bolender Center today. The polychrome exuberance and the elements and compositional expressions of movement in the Bolender Center recall John Johansen's Mummers Theater (1970) in Oklahoma City. They share an aesthetic based on common and readily available materials that have qualities that are only suggested in their most common and conventional applications.

Architecture is best in the immediacy of experience, up close, in, around and through. Movement of the body in architectural space, what Swiss-born, Paris-based architect Le Corbusier referred to as *promenade architecturale*, is the choreography of experience and requires more than the nominal stair or ramp. This is one of the many compelling aspects of the architecture of the Bolender Center, immediately apparent when one enters the great public space of arrival. The tactile qualities of space are as important as the visual, often more so, and the kinesthetic experience is significant as it certainly should be in the artistic quarters and daily lives of dancers, dance students and the many others essential to the Company and the performance of this art.

Kansas City is still very much a railroad city. In their studios, standing at the barre while practicing, dancers may watch passing trains against the backdrop of the Kansas City skyline. The Power House lost its great stack many years ago, and with it a bit of its landmark presence in the city skyline. If not quite so visibly, it is far more culturally significant in its current incarnation with the power of ballet within.

Architecture of consequence, like education, great art or a good book, is imprinted upon us, fuels our imagination, connects us to things we might never have known or experienced, or connects us more deeply to the places we live.

HOLISTIC ADAPTATION

John G. Waite, FAIA

My experience with the Kansas City Union Station is closely linked to the adjacent Liberty Memorial, constructed in 1925-26 to commemorate World War I. In 2000, our firm was asked by the Kansas City Board of Parks, Recreation, and Boulevards to participate in the restoration design and develop the historic structure, historic landscape, and preservation planning reports for the memorial. As part of that work we explored the relationship between the memorial and Union Station, which was the third largest railroad station in the United States (behind New York's Pennsylvania Station and Grand Central Terminal). Together these two structures form one of the most significant *City Beautiful* urban complexes in the nation. An integral component of the complex, and the last to be renewed, is the original Power House, now the Bolender Center.

BNIM's skillful adaptation of the Power House to serve a radically different function is a case study of successful adaptive use. Its design marks the confluence of two significant historic-preservation movements of the late twentieth century. The first is industrial archeology, a field that originated in Britain after World War II as major industrial and engineering buildings and sites were threatened with demolition as industrialization diminished. At the same time in the United States, there was a growing interest in studying and preserving industrial and engineering structures. This movement was solidified in the 1970s when the Society for Industrial Archeology (SIA) and the Historic American Engineering Record of the National Park Service (HAER) were established. Since then, many former industrial buildings have been preserved for new uses and have served as armatures for the revitalization of entire cities such as Lowell, Massachusetts.

The second significant movement is the appropriate rehabilitation of historic buildings brought about by the passage of the National Historic Preservation Act of 1966, and the development of *The Secretary of the Interior's Standards for the Treatment of Historic Properties* a decade later. Before 1966, preservationists focused mainly on individual buildings associated with important historic events or personages, many of which were museums or residences. After 1966, whole groups of buildings and districts as well as structures of all kinds were identified for preservation and incorporated into the everyday life of communities. Early reuse projects often focused on the exteriors, with little done to preserve significant interiors. *The Secretary of the Interior's Standards* discouraged this "gut and blast" approach. Instead, buildings were to be approached holistically, so that character-defining features would be identified and incorporated into the renewal process. The Bolender Center project is an example of how to study and analyze a building so that its significant features and spatial volumes are preserved while it is transformed to serve a new function.

Over the course of its lifetime, a building may have several, or even many, uses. Modern historic-preservation practice recognizes that it is important not to make irreversible modifications to essential elements that contribute to a building's basic character. This approach will ensure that it will survive extensive modifications, while retaining its basic integrity and cultural meaning for successive generations. The Bolender Center successfully follows this approach. It should serve as a model for many years to come for others to follow with buildings that present similar challenges. People will want to visit it not only for the dance programs, but to experience the architecture as well.

UNION PASSENGER STATION POWER HOUSE

Cydney Millstein

Constructed at the onset of WWI was Union Station, an imposing terminal designed in the *Beaux-Arts* tradition by Chicago architect Jarvis Hunt (1859-1941), during the grand phase of American railroad architecture. The Kansas City Terminal Railway, an operation of twelve separate railway companies, commissioned Hunt who prevailed over such architects as Daniel H. Burnham in the competition.[1] Hunt's 850,000-square-foot T-shaped station, with its soaring 95-foot-high grand lobby and a 352-foot-long main waiting room and concourse, replaced an outdated Second Empire-styled Union Avenue Depot dating from 1878 and sited in the city's West Bottoms.

Hunt's scheme for Kansas City's Union Station, hailed as "one of the most comprehensive railway terminal developments ever undertaken in this county,"[2] called for several ancillary structures: the Adams Express Building, the Railway Express Building and the Power House, the latter of which was historically referred to as Union Passenger Station Power House. As it stands today, the complex provides an intact composition of distinct property types that illustrate Kansas City's position as a key player in the nation's expanding railroads during the early decades of the 20th century.

Nephew of the celebrated New York architect Richard Morris Hunt and muralist William Morris Hunt, Jarvis Hunt was trained at Harvard and the Massachusetts Institute of Technology in the tradition of the *Ecole des Beaux-Arts*. Hunt, a Vermont native, moved to Chicago in 1893 to supervise construction of the Vermont State Building at the World's Columbian Exposition. Hunt maintained his office in Chicago for nearly thirty-five years. His practice included the design of a variety of building types from luxury residences to commercial buildings, train stations and warehouses. Significant works by Hunt include The Lake Shore Athletic Club (Chicago, 1924; now part of Northwestern University); the original buildings at the Great Lakes Naval Training Center (North Chicago, 1901-1911), several prominent *Beaux-Art* railroad stations, displaying similar characteristics to that of Union Station, to include those in Oakland, California; Joliet, Illinois; and Dallas, Texas—all completed between 1912-1916. In Kansas City, Hunt's Union Station and associated buildings, the Kansas City Star Building (1911) and the National Bank of Commerce (1906-1908), add to the list of his more outstanding works. Charles Bohasseck, key to the design of Kansas City's Union Station complex, became Hunt's business partner.[3]

previous page Distant view of Union Station, looking northwest. 1938.
right Crowd on Pershing Road at the Liberty Memorial Dedication, November 1, 1921. Union Station at right; Power House with stack in center, background. View facing west.

4793

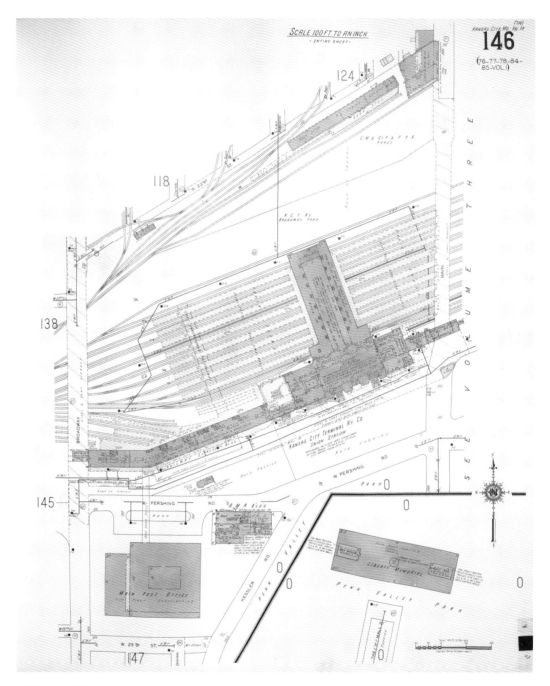

left Grand Hall, Union Station, 1915.
top Footprint of Union Station, railyards, associated structures and surrounding buildings.
Source: *Sanborn Insurance Map, Kansas City, MO.* (New York: Sanborn Map Company, 1939-1949), Vol. 1A, plate 146.

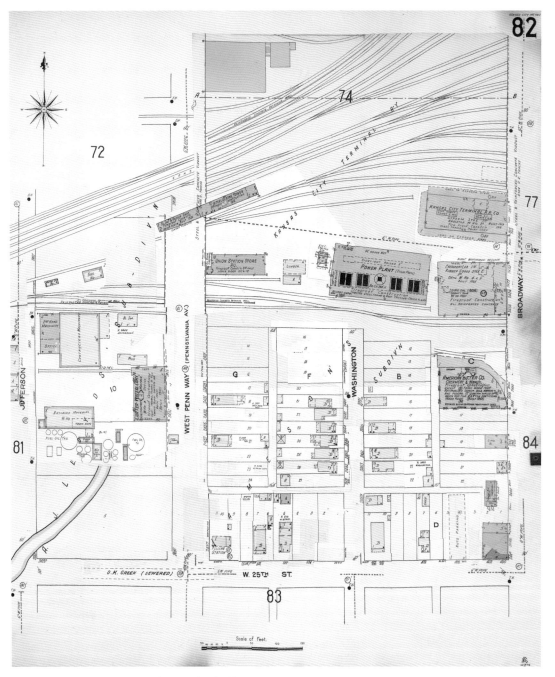

top Footprint of the Power House and surrounding buildings.
Source: *Sanborn Insurance Map, Kansas City, MO.* (New York: Sanborn Map Company, 1909-1938), Vol. 1A, plate 82.
right Aerial view of Downtown Kansas City taken near 23rd Street and Southwest Boulevard. Union Station, Power House (outlined), rail yards and associated structures, in foreground. View facing north, northeast.

Along with Union Station, the associated structures are listed in the National Register of Historic Places and have been thoughtfully renovated using *The Secretary of the Interior's Standards* as guidelines. Today, the entire complex stands revitalized in the midst of one of Kansas City's most important collections of significant landmarks—all expressions of the *City Beautiful* Movement—interlaced with early portions of Kansas City's renowned park and boulevard system by the landscape architect George Edward Kessler who espoused the same ideals for civic growth and enhancement beginning in 1893. To the south of Union Station is Liberty Memorial, a National Historic Landmark that houses the America's World War One Museum, as designated by U. S. Congress in 2004. In addition, the National Register-listed United States Main Post Office Building, turned IRS facility, completes the expansive and distinguished streetscape flanking Pershing Road.

1	Todd Bolender Center	8	National Archives and Records Administration
2	Union Station	9	Union Station Parking Garage
3	Freighthouse Pedestrian Bridge	10	Science City
4	IRS KC Service Center	11	Pershing Building
5	US Post Office	12	Liberty Lofts
6	Liberty Memorial	13	Bloch Fountain
7	Freighthouse Flats		

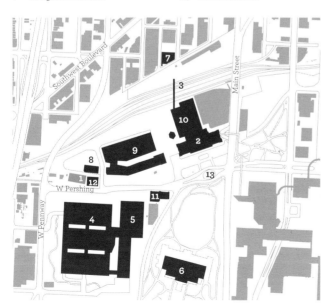

The Liberty Bell, carried on a special flat car, as it appeared at Union Station in 1915. The Power House is shown at the left of the tracks. View facing west. The reverse of the photograph reads "Famous Liberty Bell in Kansas City, W. Malcom Lowry."

Placed at a steep incline, thereby accessed at varying grades, the Power House, executed in the Classical Revival style, originally provided heat, light and power for Union Station and the associated rail yard buildings, as well as the neighboring Liberty Memorial and United States Post Office. A series of sub-basement level tunnels created below-grade access and power supply connection between these otherwise distinct and separate buildings. The four-story brick Power House, articulated with contrasting concrete belt coursing, inlaid brick and terra-cotta panels, a wide terra-cotta tile cornice and vast industrial fenestration at all façades, also supplied live steam for trains waiting in the station.[4] A penthouse, sited at the south end, is all but hidden by a tall parapet capped in terra-cotta. A 250-foot flue and smokestack, measuring 14 feet in diameter at its base and resting above the boiler room floor, was partially removed in 1975.

The scale of the Power House had to adapt to the equipment that it housed. In order to accommodate huge machinery, the interior of the Power House was originally designed with a single east-west, brick-faced partition dividing the 195-foot-long long building lengthwise at its center. Staggered levels, reached by various gallery floors and stairs, included 1) the boiler room basement 2) the engine room basement 3) the boiler room and 4) the engine room.

It would be an oversight not to mention that Hunt, in designing the complex, worked closely with John V. Hanna, chief engineer for the Terminal Railway Company and his staff of 180 employees including building, electrical, signal and division engineers, in organizing the ideal arrangement of convenience and economy of design, as well as ample combustion space. Twenty-four hours a day, seven days a week, the machinery of the Power House was in constant motion where coal, delivered by rail, was dumped into basement hoppers, then moved by conveyors to the top of the building to eight overhead coal storage hoppers, then fed back down to the boilers at the heart of the building. Coal ash was dumped into ash hoppers located below the boilers.

IT APPEARS THAT THE SAME CONVEYOR SYSTEM BROUGHT COAL ASH FROM THE BASEMENT FURNACES AND DUMPED INTO TWO OVERHEAD ASH HOPPERS LOCATED BETWEEN THE COAL BUNKERS ABOVE THE BOILER ROOM FLOOR.[5] SEEING AND HEARING THE POWER HOUSE PERFORM MIGHT HAVE BEEN DESCRIBED AS AN INDUSTRIAL CONCERTO.

In the design of any power plant, each installation is unique to the requirements and in the case of the Power House, an additional challenge was that the change in grade offset the height of each room. The boiler room basement originally contained fine coal hoppers and ash pits located below the boiler room level. The grandest of the spaces in the Power House was the boiler room, as it measured 50 feet in height and extended the entire length of the building. Eight coal furnaces, a boiler and flue system characterized this mammoth space. Each boiler was aligned with a metal coal chute that punctuated the boiler room roof at each of the eight center bays of the building. One of the most distinctive features of the room, which generated water, electricity and steam heat for the complex and surrounding buildings, is the circular brick flue, with a 14-foot diameter stack originally extending 250 feet through the roof and penthouse. It now measures 38 feet in height due to the removal of the stack above the roof.

Coal bunkers, placed above each of the coal furnaces, sat in the penthouse that maintained a capacity of 100 tons of coal for each boiler. Coal was delivered by rail, then by inner conveyors to the bunkers where the coal was processed through the furnace below.[6]

Electrical power was supplied through tunnels leading to the rail yards and the terminal's head house from the engine room basement. Located above the boiler room floor was the Engine Room, measuring 43 feet wide. Hunt's design for this section of the Power House included, at its center, a continuous Texas skylight used for mainly for ventilation.[7] An electronically operated 195-foot Gantry crane, supported by a steel frame and truss system, was also placed in the Engine Room in order to handle massive equipment about the space, in the event that additional equipment was needed or existing machinery had to be moved for repair.

In 1929, *Architectural Forum* dedicated a series of articles on the significance of power stations, saying that historically,

"THERE IS NOTHING THAT HAS REMOTELY PARALLELED THESE STRUCTURES IN USE OR DESIGN... THERE IS A FEELING OF GRANDEUR AND OF POETRY AND OF BEAUTY IN THE ORDERLY ASSEMBLY... AND IT ACTS AS A STIMULANT AND AN INSPIRATION TO THE DESIGNER OF THE STRUCTURE WHICH HOUSES IT."[8]

The Power House, while scaled and defined for the complex for which it originally served, aptly reveals Des Grange's musing about these dignified industrial structures.

Now occupied by the Kansas City Ballet, the Power House greatly retains its original integrity of design, expression and contextual relationship to the vast Union Station complex. In 2010-2011, BNIM Architects - Kansas City, skillfully restored the feeling of permanence and strength in design of this vanishing property type.

Everyone should dance.
Everyone should make music.
Each day without music
drains a drop from the soul.

BUILDING A FIRM FOOTING

TIMELINE

In its hundred-year history, the Union Station Power House has experienced a Bell curve of activity, first functioning in its intended role to power the Union Station campus, then sitting abandoned for decades, and now experiencing revitalization in its second life as the new home for Kansas City Ballet. The building, in its reincarnation, wears this history with enduring dignity and strong connections to its past.

Studies Conducted to Renovate Power House for Hotel, Brewery, Retail, Condominiums and Offices

1914   **1915**   **1970**   **1975**   **1990**   **1995**

Construction of
Jarvis Hunt Design

Power House Abandoned

Smokestack Removed

11/05
Conceptual Cost Estimate

08/28/11 - 09/02/11
Grand Opening Celebration

08/02/2011
Final Completion

2005   2006   2007   2008   2009   2010   2011

06/06
Preliminary Test Fits

04/07
Schematic Design Begins

12/09
Full Construction,
Demolition, Abatement

04/11
Topping Out

01 VISION

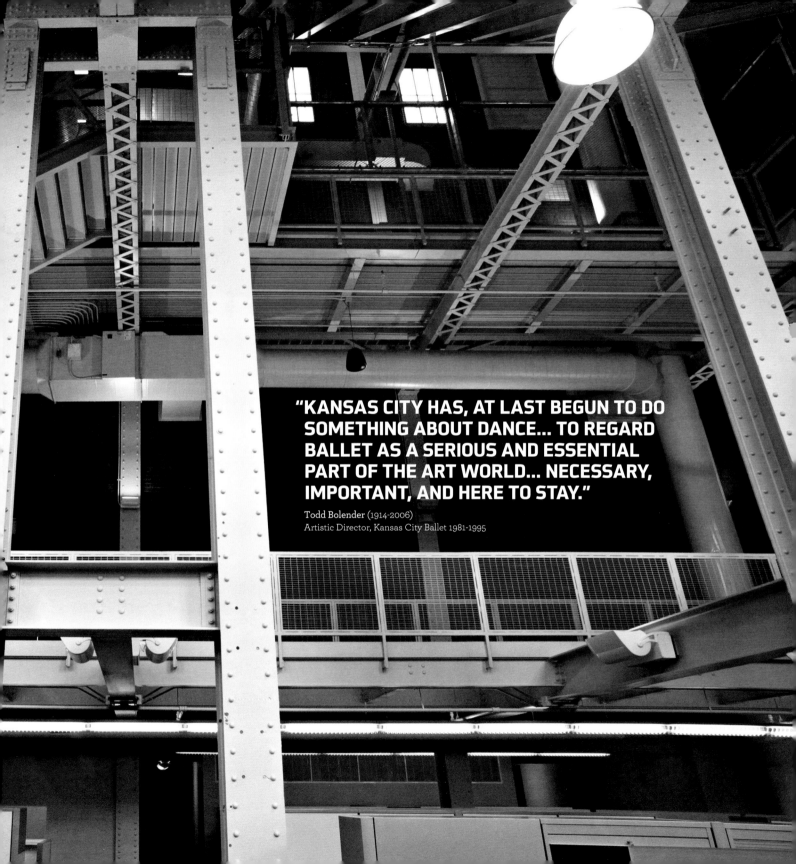

"KANSAS CITY HAS, AT LAST BEGUN TO DO SOMETHING ABOUT DANCE... TO REGARD BALLET AS A SERIOUS AND ESSENTIAL PART OF THE ART WORLD... NECESSARY, IMPORTANT, AND HERE TO STAY."

Todd Bolender (1914-2006)
Artistic Director, Kansas City Ballet 1981-1995

"WHAT A BUILDING DOES MATTERS AS MUCH AS HOW IT LOOKS."

Rodolphe el-Khoury and Andrew Payne

A few years ago, in a book written about one of BNIM's projects, the phrase *generous pragmatism* was created by el-Khoury and Payne. We were intrigued and honored by what they were observing and have come to accept it as a clear understanding of how we approach design and how our buildings perform as comfortable, welcoming and inspiring environments for people. The Jarvis Hunt design for the Power House layered with the BNIM design for the Bolender Center stands as a testament to the idea of generous pragmatism.

In its original use, the Power House was about refining energy from one source to another—coal to steam and electricity. The building was the high-performing theater or factory, depending upon your point of view. It performed those tasks with elegance and respect for the people working inside and operating the equipment. Daylight and natural ventilation systems were integral to the design and modulated the environment during winter and summer.

Today, the energy is different. The hard work and creative energy of dancers, young and old, is the refined energy, but once again the building is fulfilling its role in refinement of raw energy and power into something very precious and beautiful.

The building does its work by creating space that is day-lit, generous, comfortable, quiet when it needs to be, loud sometimes and always inspiring. The building has a lot more to do—make people comfortable and happy, fulfill many other needs from dressing rooms to wardrobe and create a community for the company and school.

BEAUTY
There are many thoughts about what makes a building like the Bolender Center beautiful. Certain tenets define beauty in ways that apply to the new dance facility. One is that buildings should touch our senses. In the case of the Bolender Center, we think of the quietness that is often contrasted by the sounds of dancers moving across a studio floor and music floating through the spaces; how daylight fills the volumes of space; or the beauty of the juxtaposed tactile surfaces of old and new materials.

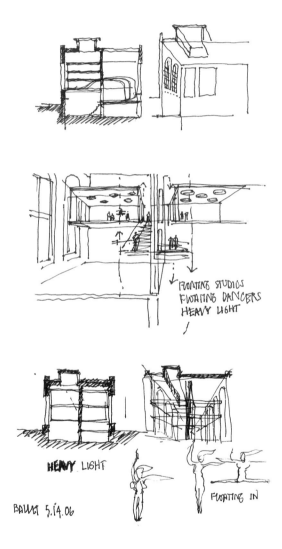

A second tenet is that the building—original Hunt design and new interventions—inspires mental or intellectual engagement that is pleasurable and interesting. The original building exhibits handsome proportions, rich materials and tectonics and spatial qualities that are remarkably humane given the original purpose. The Ballet's interventions purposefully interact with the existing architecture and place new structure and other elements to complement Hunt's design while clearly introducing the new functionality and use for a much larger and diverse human population.

COMMUNITY

Kansas Citians are always ready for a challenge. It may be a product of the condition that, as a community, we are often overlooked or, more literally, flown over when people are seeking art, creativity, innovation and beauty. However, this is changing, and Kansas City Ballet is very much part of that shift. Nonetheless, we continue to believe that we must outlive the past and work harder and more creatively to move forward in the world of art and in many other places. Some might say that is the Kansas City Spirit.

The Todd Bolender Center for Dance & Creativity is both rooted and elevated by its Kansas City Spirit. This is not something new for the Ballet; it is a part of the legacy created by the founder Tatiana Dokoudovska, redefined by Todd Bolender and alive and thriving under the leadership of William Whitener, Jeffrey J. Bentley, the current company and staff, the board and supporters.

The Bolender Center embodies the Kansas City Spirit. Its roots as part of Union Station are emblematic of our forbears' vision and spirit in placing Kansas City at the center of rail in the United States. Even today, the tracks north of the Bolender Center are the second-busiest rail freight right-of-way in the U.S.

The Bolender Center works hard to ensure that what happens inside its walls elevates the hard work and creativity of the dancers to even greater heights in the world of dance and art. They consulted with a realtor, Bryan W. Johnson of Grubb & Ellis | The Winbury Group, who presented dozens of available properties across the Kansas City area.

02 PROCESS

"VERY EARLY IN THE PROCESS WE REALIZED THAT THIS WAS NOT JUST ABOUT TRANSFORMING AN IMPORTANT BUILDING. IT WAS ALSO ABOUT A NEW ENERGY, A TRANSFORMATIONAL ENERGY THAT WILL PROPEL THIS BUILDING AND IN MANY WAYS THE ARTS AND CULTURE OF KANSAS CITY INTO THE NEXT 100 YEARS. THE OLD ENERGY WAS COAL THAT MOVED THROUGH THE BUILDING TO POWER UNION STATION AND THE PRECINCT. THE NEW ENERGY IS A CREATIVE POWER THAT IS THE PRODUCT OF THE STUDENTS AND PROFESSIONAL DANCERS—BEAUTY, CREATIVITY AND ART."

Stephen McDowell
Director of Design, BNIM

TRANSFORMATION

Approaching its 50th anniversary, Kansas City Ballet (KCB) entered the new millennium in search of a permanent home for its professional dance company and school. Its vision was to develop not just a space for teaching and rehearsing dance, but rather an incubator for creativity with potential to become a community asset as well.

Among the options that emerged from the company's search was a seemingly forgotten and rapidly declining structure just a few blocks from the site of Kansas City's new world-class performing arts center—the old abandoned Union Station Power House. Completed in 1914, the Power House provided coal-powered, steam-generated electricity and heat to the Union Station complex until it was vacated in the 1970s.

EVEN IN DECLINE, THE BUILDING SAT QUIETLY NOBLE—A TESTAMENT TO THE SKILLED HAND OF THE BUILDING'S ORIGINAL DESIGNER, CELEBRATED ARCHITECT JARVIS HUNT.

Located in one of Kansas City's most historic urban areas, the Power House was the final building in the Union Station complex to be restored. Even in its state of deterioration, the building embodied a glimmer of promise for the vision and programmatic needs of KCB. It had sufficient parking. It was filled with light. And its original industrial purpose provided an open, voluminous space awaiting something new.

To explore its vision, KCB approached BNIM with a solicitation to perform a series of test fits to assess how well the desired studio spaces, offices and necessary support spaces would fit into the shell of the Power House.

For years, BNIM had looked at the historic, deteriorating Power House facility for a variety of uses—including a potential location for the firm's headquarters. Beginning in the mid-1990s, BNIM had also been working on the ongoing renovation of Union Station and was deeply involved in the first steps of renovating the neighboring historic Railway Express and Main Post Office buildings.

This familiarity with the building and site gave the BNIM team reason to embark on the opportunity with both enthusiasm and caution.

BNIM INTERNATIONAL OFFICES @ POWER HOUSE

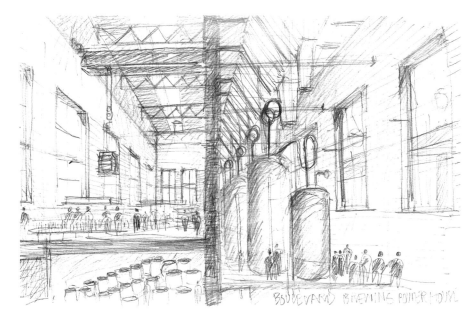

BOULEVARD BREWING POWER HOUSE

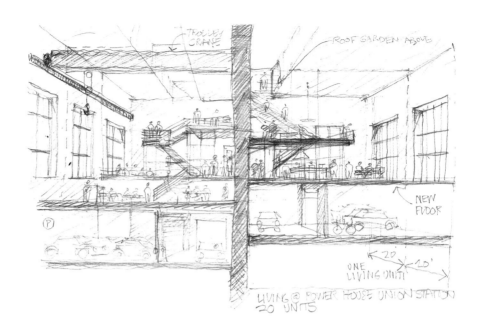

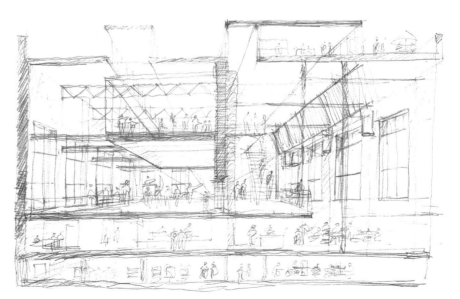

During the 1990s, BNIM performed separate studies on the abandoned Power House facility to analyze feasibility of various potential tenant uses. Scenarios included a hotel, brewery, sporting-goods retailer, condominiums, and even a possible new home for the firm.

The team first modeled the Power House using 3-D modeling software. The virtual model enabled them to nimbly execute test fits using a building program that had recently been developed for another potential site.

VERY QUICKLY THEY DISCOVERED THAT WITH THE ADDITION OF NEW FLOOR PLATES, KCB'S PROGRAM WAS A NEARLY PERFECT FIT WITHIN THE POWER HOUSE VOLUME.

———

To understand a detailed scope of a full-building rehabilitation, the team retained the services of Structural Engineering Associates (SEA) to perform a comprehensive survey of the building's existing conditions. SEA's findings were not surprising, but they presented a daunting climb ahead. Rehabilitation would include an intensive and comprehensive reinforcement to the building's structural elements, replacement of concrete, a new roof, and major repairs to masonry, terra-cotta detailing and fenestration.

From the outset of the project, a predominant goal of this effort, for everyone involved, was to restore the historic Power House to its original condition. As part of the Union Station complex, the building embodied an important story of national significance, and both KCB leadership and the BNIM design team recognized the need to honor its history.

The project team solicited the services of Architectural & Historical Research, LLC, a Kansas City-based cultural resources consulting firm led by historian Cydney Millstein. KCB was not the first organization to approach Millstein about an adaptive reuse of the Power House, but from her informed perspective, theirs was the best approach. It was a beautiful and respectful fit.

Due to the severely deteriorated conditions of the building, it was beneficial to create perspectives of the new spaces and create video walk-throughs to help the stakeholders see beyond the decay and visualize the full potential of the power house as viable project.

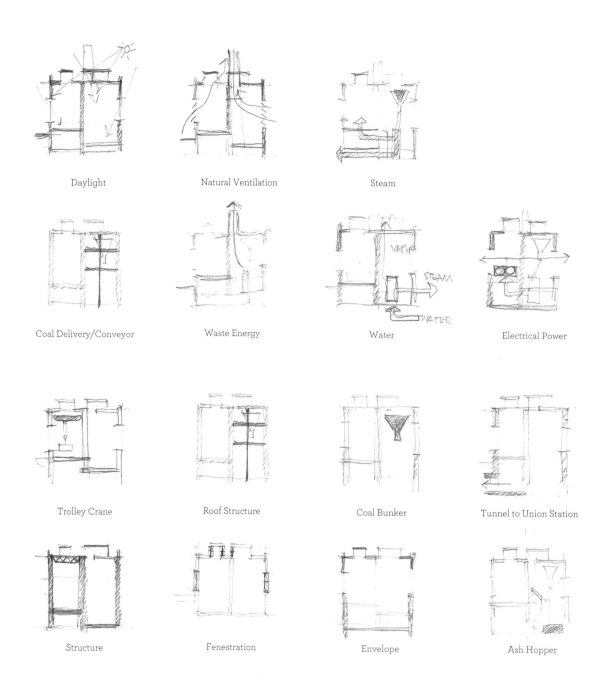

Daylight

Natural Ventilation

Steam

Coal Delivery/Conveyor

Waste Energy

Water

Electrical Power

Trolley Crane

Roof Structure

Coal Bunker

Tunnel to Union Station

Structure

Fenestration

Envelope

Ash Hopper

LAYERS OF DESIGN: Existing Systems and Architectural Features

Earlier, in 2004, Millstein had led the efforts to place the Power House—along with two other Union Station ancillary buildings, Adams Express and Railway Express—in the National Register of Historic Places. Millstein understood that from the perspective of the National Park Service and *The Secretary of the Interior's Standards for the Treatment of Historic Properties*—a federal guideline of how to treat historic properties in order to achieve historic tax credits—the Power House embodied tremendous historic significance. Not only were there architectural elements to preserve, but the volumes of space also became an interesting consideration.

Concurrent with the structural and rehabilitation evaluations, the design team worked with owner and user groups to delineate the detailed functional needs of the building's spaces. Through an engagement process that involved many meetings of the board, parent committees, professional dancers and staff, BNIM gained a much deeper insight into the needs of the new facility. Meetings of the core design and client team were supplemented with Saturday and evening sessions to share the design concept with the larger group of stakeholders and to solicit feedback. Very thoughtful suggestions ran the gamut, from dancer experience, to places for parents to make their waiting time useful, to accommodations for students doing schoolwork, to exhibition space for archives, to insuring a well-organized and safe student pick up area.

IT WAS THROUGH THIS PROCESS THAT THE DESIGN EVOLVED FROM A DETAILED SPACE PROGRAM AND HISTORIC BUILDING INTO THE NEW HOME FOR DANCE AND CREATIVITY.

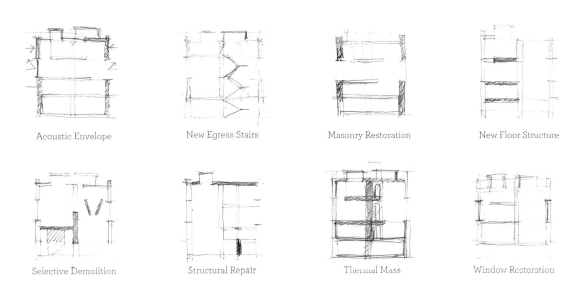

Acoustic Envelope   New Egress Stairs   Masonry Restoration   New Floor Structure

Selective Demolition   Structural Repair   Thermal Mass   Window Restoration

LAYERS OF DESIGN: Process

Construction kicked off with an entire year focused on remediation, demolition and removal of debris. The demolition and construction team, including JE Dunn Construction, DECO Companies and Kingston Environmental, coordinated this potentially hazardous process with efficiency and success. They safely removed asbestos, lead paint and tons of concrete and steel. Simultaneously, they began reinforcing the building's structural elements and preparing its armature to support a new purpose.

From the beginning, everything was done right.

THE DESIGN AND CONSTRUCTION TEAM APPROACHED THE POWER HOUSE RESTORATION WITH THE BELIEF THAT ANYTHING DONE TO BRING THIS HISTORIC BUILDING BACK INTO REUSE SHOULD MAINTAIN A SENSE OF THE BUILDING'S ORIGINAL USE.

———

This building in its restored form is overwhelmingly historic. Even though the building clearly houses KCB, one could tour it today and, with minimal explanatory dialogue, understand its former use.

FINANCING THE VISION
The realization of the new Todd Bolender Center for Dance & Creativity was made possible by two critical financial provisions: a generous endowment from the Muriel McBrien Kauffman Foundation and substantial historic preservation tax credits. Famously generous in the state of Missouri, the availability of tax credits became a driving factor in the decision to transform the Power House into a new home for KCB.

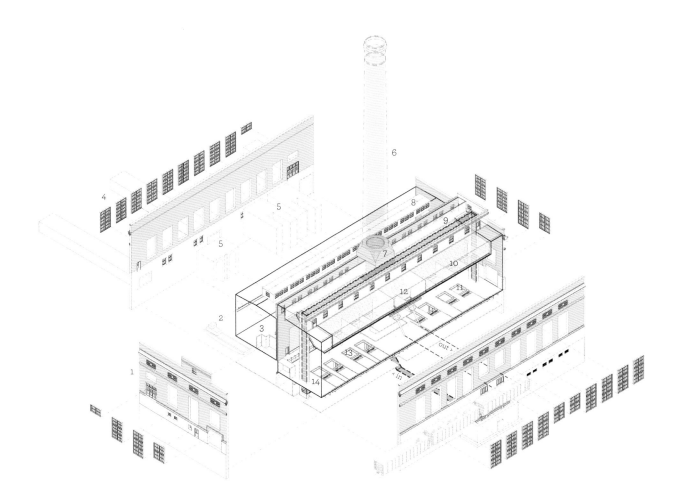

EXISTING BUILDING (above)

1   Brick Masonry, Terra-cotta and Concreate
2   Gantry Crane
3   Engine Room
4   Historic Windows
5   Concrete Platforms for Engine Room Equipment
6   Former Chimney
7   Chimney Base
8   "Texas" Skylight
9   Penthouse
10 Coal Bunkers
11 Boiler Locations
12 Ash Hoppers
13 Boiler Room
14 Conveyor System

NEW BUILDING (right)

A   Main Entrance and Canopy
B   Entrance
C   Vertical Circulation
D   Basement
E   Planting Beds
F   Gantry Crane
G   Performance Studio
H   Floating Small Practice Studios
I   Replaced "Texas" Skylight
J   Skylight and Relief Air

K   Suspended Circulation thru
    Chimney Vault
L   Large Pratice Studios
M   Mechanical Platform
N   Dock Platform
O   Open Offices
P   Children's Dressing Areas
Q   Lobby
R   Lightcourt
S   Exitway

Existing Volumes   Public Spaces   New Spaces

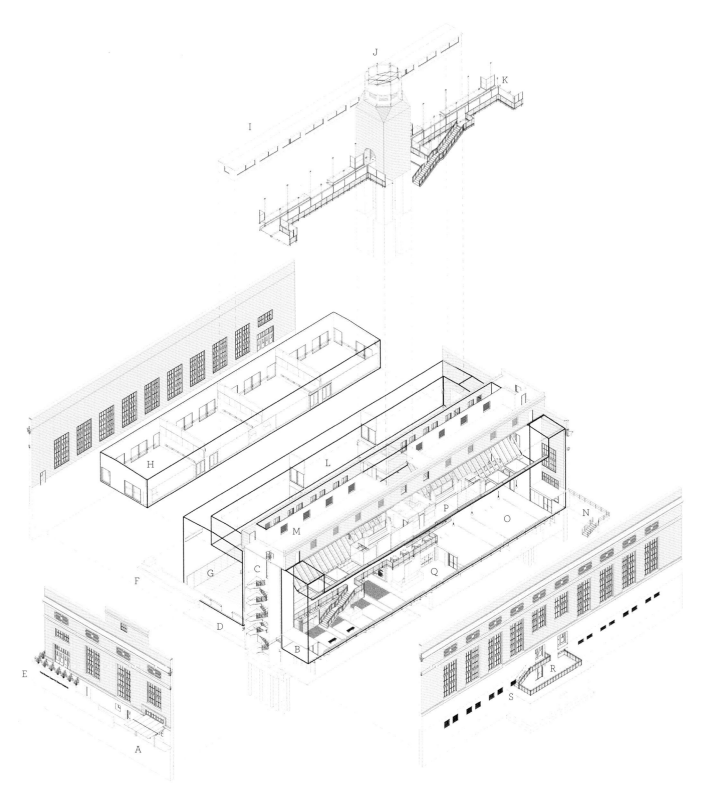

VISIONARY DESIGN SCENARIOS

The Power House's original smokestack structure was demolished in 1975, leaving the design team with an unresolved chimney base opening that presented an opportunity for an iconic solution. During conceptual design, BNIM considered several visionary design scenarios for the truncated chimney base.

One option proposed using the base as a platform for a vertical wind turbine tower, which would have created on-site renewable energy. The site was located in a low-wind zone, so turbine design leaned toward vertical options that required less wind to operate. Even though the existing structure had supported massive weight at one time, vibration and noise mitigation, structural costs and product development realities for the turbine option proved cost prohibitive.

The project team also explored potential artist collaborations. Concept discussions included wind and motion elements to create a canvas in the skyline, shimmering light from fluttering sequins.

In the end, the design team moved forward with a compact, functional solution that provides natural daylight to the interior of the building and serves as relief air for the HVAC systems of the building. The tube steel frame structure supporting the elements also supports a lightning rod at the highest point of the building. The rings of metal mesh fabric are a reference to the smokestack's original circumference, while the truncated octagon enclosure is a response to the eight-sided existing chimney base on which it sits. Its color matches that of the interior, bright and iconic in the skyline.

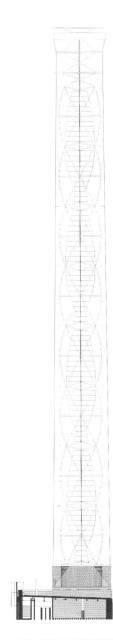

PROPOSED WIND TURBINE

CHIMNEY DEMOLISHED IN 1976

0   10'

03 DESIGN

"GRIT GIVES WAY TO GRACE.

THE GREATEST ARCHITECTURES ARE REVEALED IN SECTION AND,
NO EXCEPTION, THE BOLENDER CENTER IS ENLIVENED THROUGH
PLAN/SECTION SIMULTANEITY. PROGRAM SPACES OVERLAP,
COEXISTING IN PRESENT AND PAST. SPOLIA REMAINS, HARKENING
HISTORIC FORM-SCALE RELATIONSHIPS JUXTAPOSING THE
TYPOLOGIES OF DANCE AND ITS ATTENDANT RITUALS."

'PERHAPS TIME'S DEFINITION OF COAL IS THE DIAMOND.' K. Gibran

Tim de Noble, AIA
Professor and Dean, The College of Architecture, Planning & Design
Kansas State University

"THE PROJECT TEAM HAD THE DAUNTING TASK OF TURNING GENERATOR ROOMS INTO DANCE STUDIOS, COAL BUNKERS INTO DRESSING ROOMS, AND FIRE PITS INTO USEABLE SPACE WHILE MAINTAINING ENOUGH HISTORICAL BUILDING ASPECTS FOR THE BALLET TO EARN FEDERAL TAX CREDITS. OUR ENTIRE DESIGN, CONSTRUCTION AND CLIENT TEAM PERFORMED PRE-CONSTRUCTION PLANNING FOR OVER TWO YEARS IN ORDER TO COMPLETE THE DESIGN REQUIRED TO CONVERT THE POWER HOUSE BUILDING TO THE HOME OF KCB."

Chris Szeliga
Sr. Project Manager with general contractor, JE Dunn Construction

CONSTRAINTS & OPPORTUNITIES

Transforming the Power House into a new center for dance and creativity involved designing respectful interventions, executing painstaking restoration to each building component and creatively integrating old with new, all within stringent constraints of *The Secretary of the Interior's Standards for the Treatment of Historic Properties* guidelines. The team carefully analyzed each design decision, seeking meaningful alignment between the vision of KCB and the integrity of the building's history.

CONSTRAINTS
With the design and construction of each building component came a unique set of challenges. These challenges, or constraints, most often involved finding the solution that best balanced preservation and functional considerations.

OPPORTUNITIES
Throughout the design and construction process, the team found opportunities to explore innovative interventions, integrate sustainable solutions and deepen the historical integrity of the building's adaptive reuse.

The following pages illustrate some of the key constraints and the resulting opportunities.

01 STRUCTURE

02 INTERIOR VOLUMES

03 MICHAEL & GINGER FROST STUDIO THEATER

04 PRACTICE STUDIOS

05 CIRCULATION & SUPPORT SPACES

06 FENESTRATION

07 EXTERIOR MASONRY

08 ADAPTIVE REUSE OF MATERIALS

09 SUSTAINABLE DESIGN

01

STRUCTURE

Anyone entering the Power House was immediately struck by the massive amounts of steel framing used to support the functional elements of the building's original purpose—heavy boilers, turbine generators and coal bunkers—set against a backdrop of soaring ceilings and remnants of the power plant's operational mechanisms and simple efficiency. But the Power House had suffered severe deterioration. Over time, chemicals and heat from the coal-burning process followed by years of unchecked exposure to harsh elements had slowly eaten away at building components.

The structural state of the building and its components was of foremost concern and represented the greatest restoration challenge. The 'Texas Skylight'—raised portions of roof with operable glass windows that can be opened to release heat and allow natural sunlight to enter—had reached an advanced state of masonry wall failure due to corrosion and a flaw in the walls' original construction and needed to be replaced. Framed and structural elements showed corrosion and delamination so severe that replacement was the most economical option. Steel beams and plate girders required repair and strengthening at various levels of the building. In addition to corroded steel columns, the basement also revealed a need for replacement of all concrete components.

On the building's exterior, a complete restoration required repair and replacement of the roof, concrete, brick masonry, decorative terracotta bands, parapets and wood windows on every façade.

Meeting the guidelines in *The Secretary of the Interior's Standards* meant assessing each structural element to determine if restoration or replacement was needed. For each instance in which replacement was recommended, the team was required to prove its case and propose an appropriate and historically respectful solution.

Despite corrosion to various building components, the building's structural integrity remained relatively sound. The original function of the Power House required that its structure bear immense loads of machinery, equipment, coal and ash. Without that weight, there was a great deal of structural redundancy in the building.

This redundancy offered certain design opportunities. The amount of new steel needed was minimal. There was no need for new columns. And the structure allowed the team to insert entirely new floor plates within confines of the existing structure to increase the building's square footage.

Due to the massive amount of steel elements, the design team selected a light paint color to unify and de-emphasize all steel components while maximizing natural light levels in the upper levels of the building to create a light, airy feel. The building organization and use of fire protection allowed the team to leave the steel exposed, presenting two design opportunities: showcasing rivets and lace beam construction of the building's original construction time period, and avoiding a costly encasement in fire proofing.

The building's original structural elements also strongly informed new spatial configuration. Existing elements steered the locations of new floor plates. Rather than on one level, smaller studios were able to "float" above and within the larger studio volumes below. As one moved up in of the building, the structure made spaces more confined, leading the design team to place smaller studios on the uppermost floors for use by the smallest building users—children. Brackets used to support the formerly operational gantry crane rails became obvious locations for new steel beams to support the incoming floating studios, which were nested in the space through which the gantry crane once moved. Circulation connections in the southern half of the building aligned perfectly with existing chimney arch openings and coal bunker and ash hopper structural steel elements. The northern length of the building became evident as the primary column-free space, which exactly met the clear dimensional requirements for all the studio volumes.

02

INTERIOR VOLUMES

To accommodate huge machinery, the interior of the original Power House was essentially an open space with a single east-west partition dividing the building lengthwise along its center axis. To either side of this partition, the building's levels staggered in alignment, comprising the principal spaces: the Boiler Room along the southern half, and the Engine Room, offices and bathrooms along the northern portion.

IT WAS THESE VAST SPACES THAT EMBODIED KCB'S VISION FOR ITS NEW HOME, INCLUDING WHAT IT CALLED THE "TRINITY OF AESTHETICS" FOR ITS STUDIO SPACES—SPATIAL HEIGHT, COLUMN-FREE STUDIOS AND ABUNDANT NATURAL LIGHTING.

The primary new spaces needed to be, of course, the studios and other accommodations that directly support the professional company and the school. BNIM quickly learned, however, that the new facilities should also serve as a welcoming, highly functional venue for everyone that would interact with the facility—students, dancers, staff and parents.

In organizing the new tenant spaces, the BNIM team took great care to maintain a majority of the building's original spatial volumes—an historic preservation element that has attracted more scrutiny from the National Park Service in recent years. It was critical that the large spaces not be divided and compartmentalized beyond recognition. Originally the Power House building featured spaces with great height and width, and those volumes of space needed to remain largely intact.

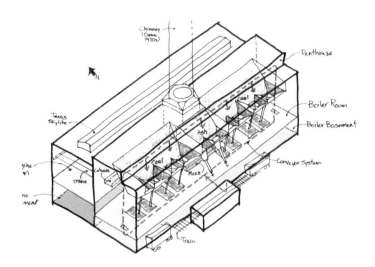

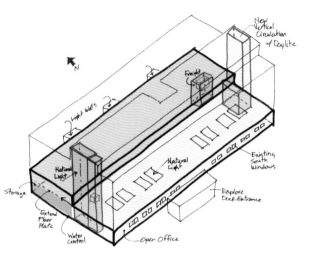

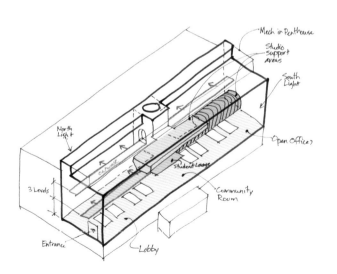

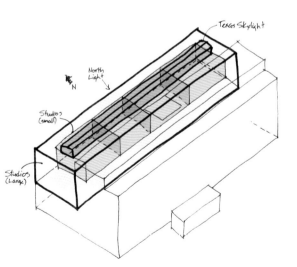

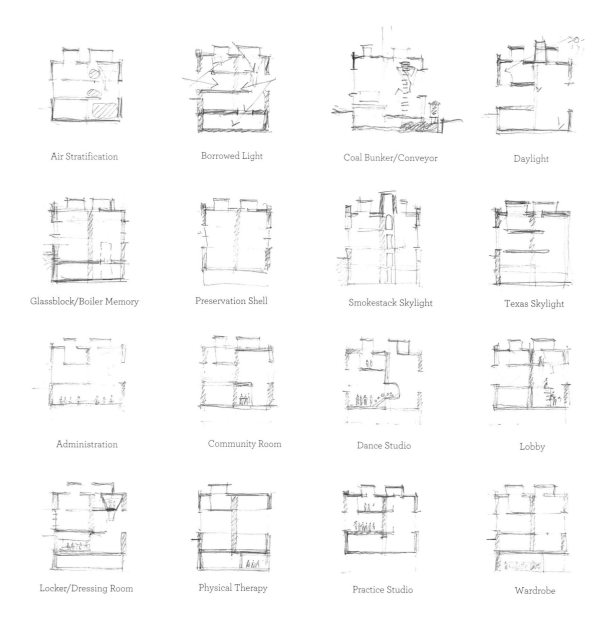

Air Stratification

Borrowed Light

Coal Bunker/Conveyor

Daylight

Glassblock/Boiler Memory

Preservation Shell

Smokestack Skylight

Texas Skylight

Administration

Community Room

Dance Studio

Lobby

Locker/Dressing Room

Physical Therapy

Practice Studio

Wardrobe

LAYERS OF DESIGN: New Systems and Architectural Spaces

THE POWER HOUSE WAS AN UNCANNY FIT FOR ITS NEW RESIDENT, AND
UNDERSTANDING THE GOALS AND VISION FOR THE BALLET WAS CRUCIAL
DURING THE DESIGN PROCESS. IN CONFIGURING THE INCOMING INTERIOR
SPACES, THE BNIM TEAM FOUND THAT THEY COULD MEET, TO PRECISE
MEASURE, EVERY PROGRAMMATIC REQUIREMENT THAT KCB HAD ORIGINALLY
DEFINED AT THE OUTSET OF THE DESIGN PROCESS. BUT IT TOOK MORE THAN
JUST SQUARE FOOTAGE TO CREATE A LASTING HOME FOR KCB.

The building's original spatial organization naturally lent itself to accommodate the programmatic needs of the company, school and staff. Though the building's existing square footage was less than what was needed to house the program, the volume and height far surpassed what was required. This naturally led the team to add new floor plates to increase square footage. Through the design team's careful attention to flow and adjacencies and clever configuration of the building's volumes, studios, offices and common spaces fell into place.

The North Engine Room, once a vast space housing tons of whirring machinery and generators, ran the length of the building's north side and rose the full height of the structure. Lined with towering windows and topped with a Texas skylight, the space generously provided the all-important "trinity of aesthetics" needed for KCB's dance studios.

The South Boiler Room presented a similarly appropriate fit for circulation, office and support spaces. In its former life, this area, comprising the south half of the Power House, had also served a circulatory function—conveying coal from a train dock on the south façade to feed eight coal bunkers that funneled into the steam generating boilers below. And in reverse, the same conveying system transported coal ash from the basement to two ash hoppers overhead.

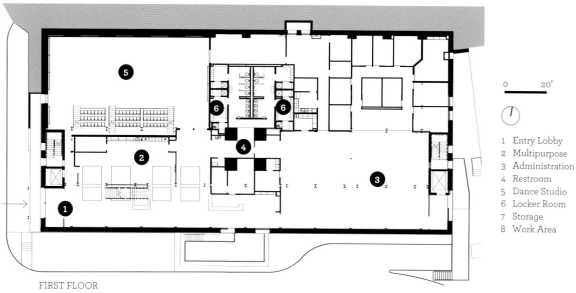

0   20'

FIRST FLOOR

1   Entry Lobby
2   Multipurpose
3   Administration
4   Restroom
5   Dance Studio
6   Locker Room
7   Storage
8   Work Area

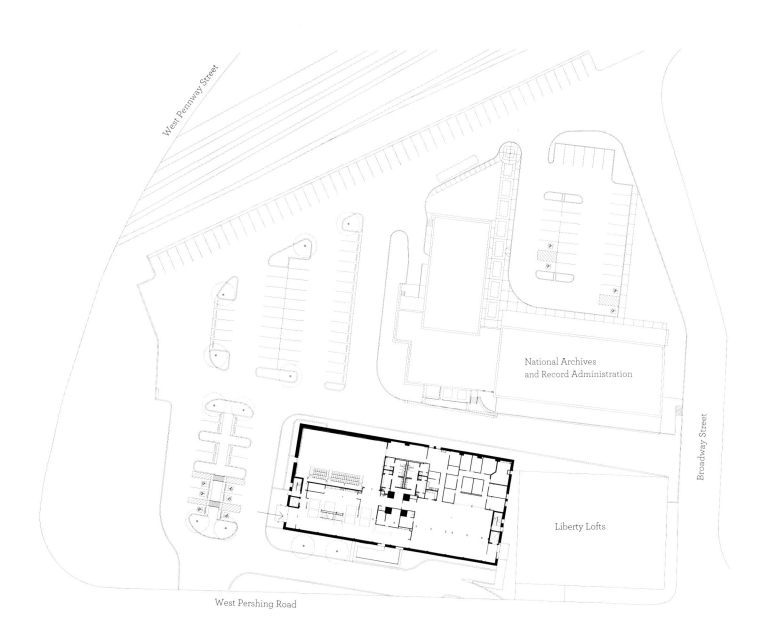

West Pennway Street

West Pershing Road

Broadway Street

National Archives
and Record Administration

Liberty Lofts

SITE PLAN

0   40'

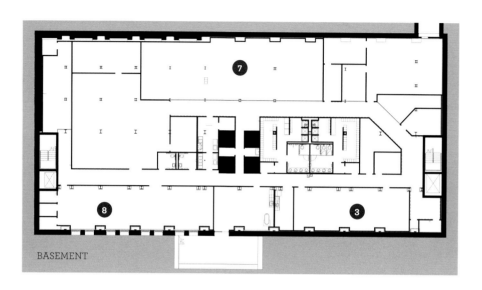

BASEMENT

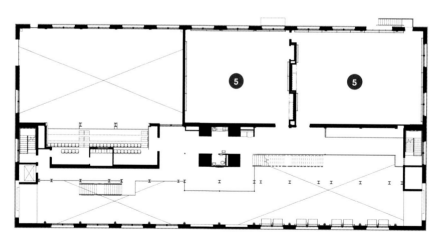

MEZZANINE

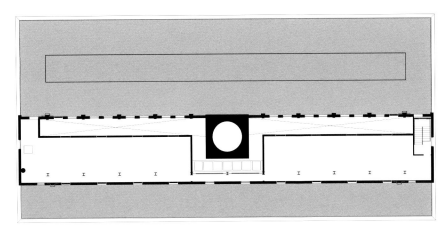

PENTHOUSE

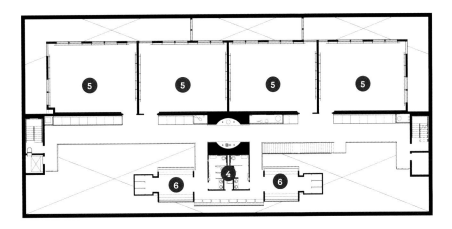

SECOND FLOOR

0   20'

1   Entry Lobby
2   Multipurpose
3   Administration
4   Restroom
5   Dance Studio
6   Locker Room
7   Storage
8   Work Area

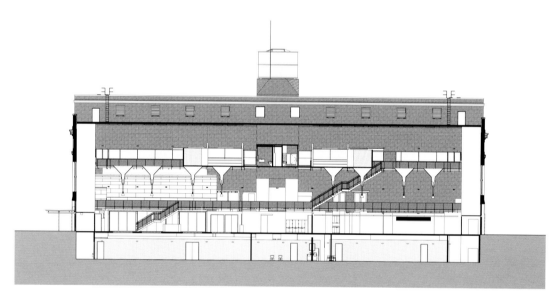

LONGITUDINAL SECTION

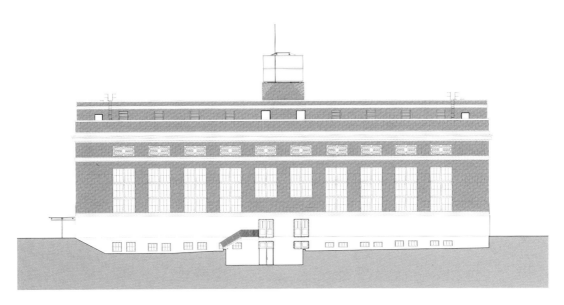

SOUTH ELEVATION

0   20'

Dividing the North Engine Room from the South Boiler Room, a massive wall of brick was punctured at strategic locations for connections between the two sides. An orange "hood" cuts through the wall, carving out volume for the 180 seats in the main performance studio.

THE ARCHITECTURE WAS PURPOSEFUL IN ENCOURAGING OPENNESS AND COMMUNITY.

Through this same brick wall, BNIM designed a pair of large portal windows connecting the public gathering areas on the mezzanine with an unobstructed view into KCB company's primary rehearsal space.

Though strongly linear and relatively easy to configure horizontally, the building presented a bigger challenge with vertical organization. The Power House was originally designed with floor plates that varied in elevation, with the north half of the building's first level sitting twelve feet higher than that of its south half. The design team toyed with a variety of schemes for configuring the north vertical space, and the process yielded a clear winner.

The team decided to drop a portion of the north floor slab by twelve feet, involving a lengthy and arduous demolition phase, but the twelve feet of additional vertical space allowed the north half of the building to fit three generous levels of studio spaces. This vertically oriented organization—totaling five levels from basement to mechanical platform in the former penthouse—strongly influenced the organization of KCB's program.

The daylight and area requirements were achieved by floating the four smaller studios above and within the larger studio volumes below. This configuration created a vertical separation between smaller and larger studios, informing the location of children areas on the second floor.

03

MICHAEL & GINGER FROST STUDIO THEATER

KCB's professional dance company presented strict programmatic needs with regard to its main rehearsal studio: the floor area needed to match the dimensions of the performance stage at the nearby performing arts center and be free of columns; height would need to accommodate choreography and staging; the space needed to be naturally day-lit; and the space should accommodate tiered seating.

Though the interior volumes and window placement of the Power House could accommodate these needs, the design team spent a great deal of time working with KCB leadership and user groups to determine the most appropriate, advantageous solutions.

Another challenge the design team faced was the existence of two original entrances to this corner of the former Engine Room—a small single door to the north, and a large dock door opening to the west. The new building configuration no longer utilized these openings as building entrances, but the need to conform to the *Interior Standards* guidelines required the team to carefully address its treatment in the façade renovation.

Located in the northeast corner of the building, the main professional studio, named the Michael & Ginger Frost Studio Theater, immediately took shape in the design process as a soaring triple-height space brought to life by daylight from windows and skylight and views to the surrounding urban environment. The placement of the building's structural columns and the linear nature of the space informed the placement of the theater's 180 seats along the south wall of the studio. A gantry crane from the building's industrial days was nested at the far the new studio theater, which met the floor area requirements to match the performance stage dimensions at the performing arts center.

A major design decision that was weighed over and over involved how the main studio would be experienced. Should it be black-box studio theater? Would patrons enter from the back of the seating directly from the lobby, or enter at dance floor level? Ultimately, the idea of a black-box space was dismissed, as it would limit the amount of daylight in the space, and entry at both the dance floor and mezzanine level were determined to ensure the most enjoyable experience. This question had many repercussions regarding the overall design, and the decision would define the patron experience, a consideration that was not taken lightly.

The team's decision to carve out the seating to the south, delicately creating a new form in the boiler room that became known as "the hood," took careful execution. This form made possible the desired orientation of the seating to the performance floor, enabling the team to maximize the floor space dedicated to the company. The seating was designed to provide an elevated vantage point for critiques and audience viewing, while a control room and storage area support studio functions.

04

PRACTICE STUDIOS

With the placement of the main Frost Studio Theater in the northeast corner of the building, the remaining six dance studios fell into place within the volume of the former North Engine Room. The design team's reconfiguration of the space required placement of new floor plates to increase square footage as needed to accommodate the new studios.

A primary design challenge became the relationship between the floor plates, studio enclosures and locations of the historic windows along the north, east and west façades of the building. The design of the smaller studios would require creatively designed interventions allowing windows and daylight to be shared between studio spaces.

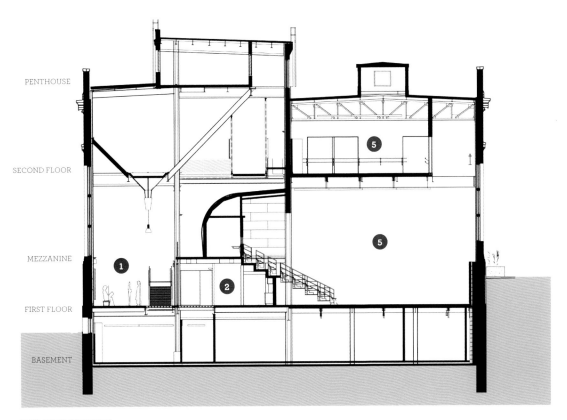

PENTHOUSE

SECOND FLOOR

MEZZANINE

FIRST FLOOR

BASEMENT

BUILDING SECTION

0   20'

1 Entry Lobby
2 Multipurpose
3 Administration
4 Restroom
5 Dance Studio

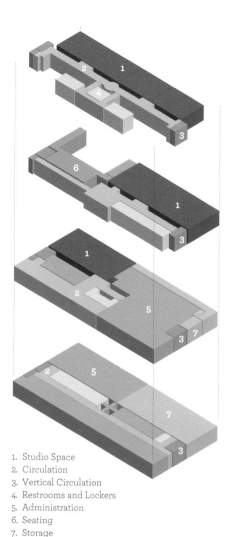

1. Studio Space
2. Circulation
3. Vertical Circulation
4. Restrooms and Lockers
5. Administration
6. Seating
7. Storage

The mezzanine level houses two spacious studios, the western-most of which offers a view looking down into the Frost Studio space below. The circulation spaces at this level are open to the soaring south half of the building and provide access to the Frost Studio seating, space for waiting and informal gathering, and a portal into the professional studio where students and visitors can observe and be inspired by the rehearsals taking place.

The second-floor studio level offers several of the building's most breathtaking moments. Maximizing the visual connections to the outdoors and the amount of northern light, a scheme was developed to share daylight from windows and skylights distributed through three levels of studio space. BNIM's design team developed a beautiful and functional "floating studio" concept that provides a band of four smaller studios inset several feet from the west, north and east walls of the building. The resulting spaces, which are wrapped in glass, mirror and white surfaces, share daylight they gain from the Texas skylight above while borrowing additional daylight from the large windows below.

05

CIRCULATION & SUPPORT SPACES

In designing circulation and support spaces within the volumes of the Power House, the design team's main challenge involved economizing space while balancing individual and privacy needs for staff, dancers, students and visitors.

As a professional dance company and school, KCB's priority was always focused on the dance studios. Thus, secondary spaces needed to fit within the confines of volumes not utilized by the studios. This posed a configuration challenge for the design team. Carefully assessing adjacencies, circulation and preservation considerations, the team studied various scenarios to maximize space while providing environments that were inviting and functional.

For KCB and School, the Power House provides 58,000 square feet of space, housing seven studios, a physical therapy suite, lockers and shower facilities for the company, a wardrobe workroom, pre-function space, the Estelle S. And Robert A. Long Ellis Conference Room, archives and office space for staff.

BNIM developed a spatial layout that kept the professional company and larger spaces at the lowest levels of the building while sending the smallest users to the top, utilized grand, open staircases to move visitors throughout, and maintained the building's openness, both visually and acoustically, to encourage interaction between user groups.

THE CATWALK CIRCULATION ALONG THE SECOND LEVEL OFFERS PERHAPS THE MOST STUNNING FEATURE IN THE BUILDING—THE FORMER POWER HOUSE CHIMNEY. ONCE A TOWERING BRICK SMOKESTACK, THE CHIMNEY WAS SHORTENED CONSIDERABLY IN THE 1970S. THE DESIGN TEAM TOPPED THE CHIMNEY WITH A CUSTOM DESIGNED GLASS CAP, TRANSFORMING THE BRICK SHAFT INTO A GLOWING, GLORIFIED SKYLIGHT, WHICH ALSO SERVES A FUNCTIONAL PURPOSE. LOUVERS AT THE PERIMETER OF THE CHIMNEY'S NEW CAP PROVIDE RELIEF AIR TO THE HVAC SYSTEMS IN THE BUILDING. ONE CAN EXPERIENCE A VERY SUBTLE AIRFLOW MOVING THROUGH THE ARCHED OPENINGS OF THE CHIMNEY AND THEN UP AND OUT THE TOP OF THE CHIMNEY—A REMINDER OF ITS FORMER FUNCTION AS A SMOKESTACK.

The south half of the building was described during board presentations as the "living room"—an open social space conducive to gatherings. It serves as a lobby, waiting area, and provides generous space for queuing and circulation. The expanded mezzanine provides an intermediate space, connected with dramatic staircases. Layering the north half of the building to house the seven studios allowed the design team to leave the south half vertically open. The former South Boiler Room creates a new public realm that is unprecedented in ballet facilities. The volume and unique structure provides organization for a new lobby, offices and circulation zones that are flooded in natural light during the day and illuminated at night by eight pendant lights integrated into the former coal bunker metal plate funnels. Tucked above the lights at the second level, unique and prominent interior sloped steel structures—former coal bunkers and ash hoppers—now serve as children's locker and dressing areas.

It is not often that an existing structure has two rows of forty-five-degree angled steel running the entire length of building, forty feet in air. BNIM's decision to repurpose these elements for use in the children's locker and dressing areas created spaces that are playful and engaging to those who make the journey to the second floor. Bleacher-style seating follows the sloped steel structure halfway up on both sides, providing some visual separation and privacy. Along the south side, bar grating finishes traveling along the sloped steel to the exterior wall, allowing filtered daylight into the dressing rooms and cutting site lines for privacy.

The building's basement, once flooded with standing water, became a valuable source of space. The design team transformed the basement spaces into locker rooms and bathrooms for the professional dancers, an expansive wardrobe workroom that is partially day-lit by the glass block flooring in the lobby above, and archives.

In administrative areas, the team designed a primarily open-office environment—a big shift for staff, who were accustomed to more isolated work spaces. A series of configuration studies yielded a balance that allowed private offices for executives and open work stations for staff.

06

FENESTRATION

The Secretary of the Interior's Standards present strict guidelines on the restoration of windows in historic buildings, which required the design and construction team to painstakingly assess each window component and determine a comprehensive approach to preserving, restoring and/or replicating the windows to their original condition, referring to the building's original drawings.

On the exterior, the building's fenestration was a primary historic element. The defining moment in the exterior articulation of the Power House—a rectangular brick building—lay in the cadence of its large, paned windows. Acknowledging their importance, the design team worked to maintain all exterior window placements and openings as Jarvis Hunt originally designed them.

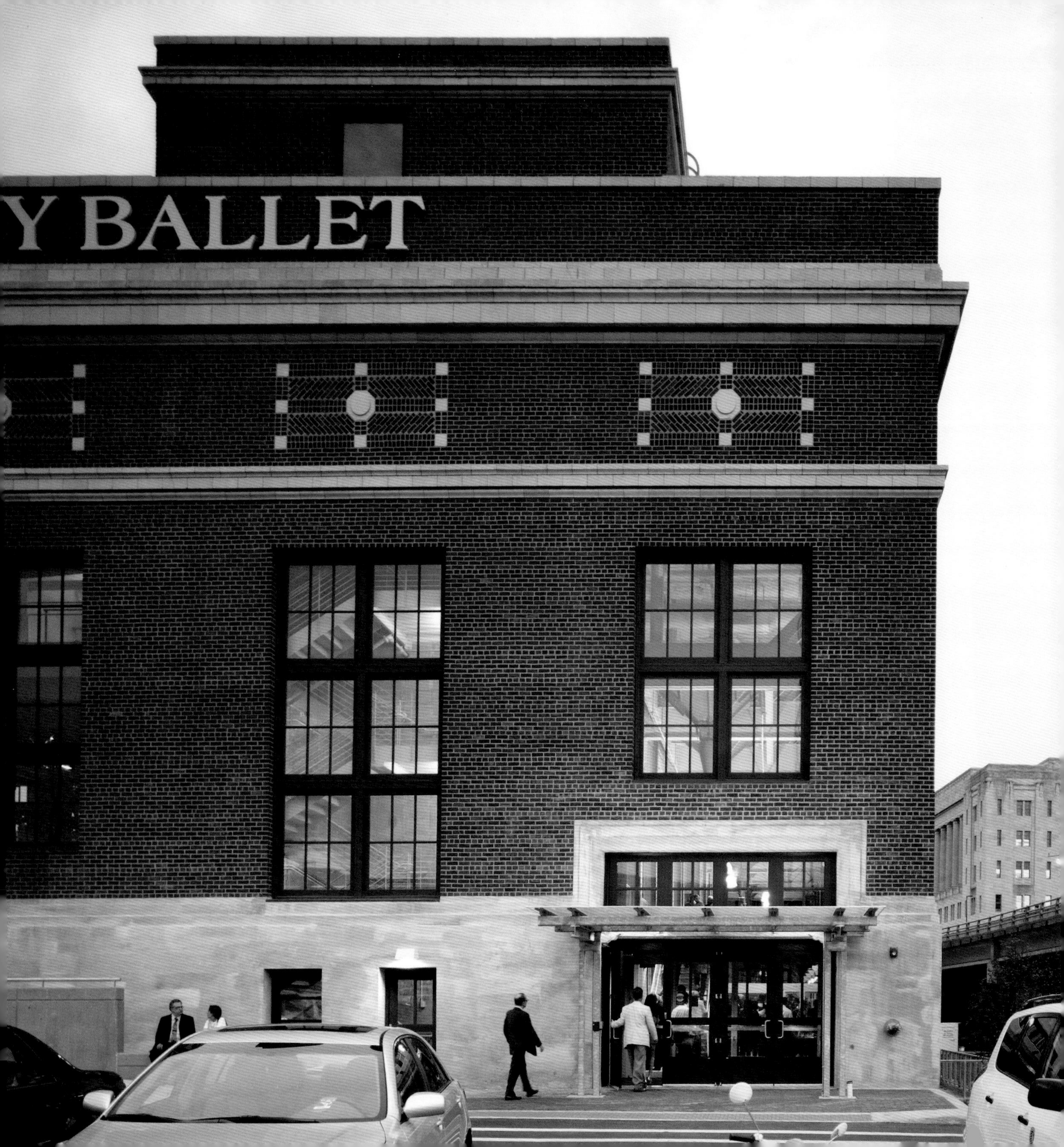
Y BALLET

In addition to maintaining original window placement, the team carefully assessed the condition of the building's original 100-year-old window frames, which they found to be in remarkably sound condition. With careful oversight, all of the building's windows were meticulously restored and/or replicated as needed, and their extraordinary match to the original windows—in profile, configuration, materials and detailing—became a source of celebration for the design team. The window restoration also presented an opportunity to introduce new sustainable Accoya-wood sashes and insulated glazing systems, which provided an energy efficient assembly while silencing adjacent train noise. Respecting both historic and modern considerations, they were a perfect fit.

In a state of structural failure, the original Texas skylight at the building's roof required a complete replacement. Taking advantage of the daylight provided by the skylight, which ran nearly the entire length of the building's north half, the design team replicated the original scale and volume using modern materials to increase performance.

07

EXTERIOR MASONRY

The exterior of the original Power House was comprised of an exposed concrete foundation, brickwork at all façades, a wide, decorative terra-cotta belt course, decorative in-laid brick and terra-cotta panels capped by a continuous terra-cotta cornice and a solid brick parapet wall shielding the roof. In a state of deterioration and structural disrepair, the façade and the building's exterior structural components posed a daunting task. Rehabilitation of the building's exterior masonry required careful consideration to aesthetics and original material composition as well as respectful attention to historical exterior components.

The construction team
removed and replaced

17,500
bricks,

268
pieces of terra-cotta and

158,000
linear feet of brick joint,

and they cleaned and sealed

134,000
square feet of brick and terracotta.

MASONRY WORK

The masonry repair on the building was an arduous endeavor and entailed careful research and testing to ensure proper restoration. The first task involved removing and replacing bricks and terra-cotta with perfect replicas. Incredibly, the project contractor, JE Dunn, was able to locate a match to the existing bricks from the original kiln and manufacturer in Bixby, Oklahoma, thereby replacing 822 damaged bricks.

The most time-consuming masonry repair involved a comprehensive tuckpointing of the exterior. JE Dunn painstakingly tested and matched the mortar to the original compound, and then raked and pointed every joint on the exterior of the building.

08

ADAPTIVE REUSE OF MATERIALS

The National Park Service emphasizes that an adaptive reuse should fit within the *Standards,* not the other way around.

WITH A COMMITTED DESIGN TEAM AND KCB LEADERSHIP IN FULL SUPPORT, NOT ONLY DID THE POWER HOUSE RESTORATION FIT WITHIN THE STANDARDS, BUT THE DESIGN TEAM ALSO FOUND WAYS TO CREATIVELY WEAVE HISTORIC ELEMENTS INTO THE DESIGN VOCABULARY OF THE TENANT'S INCOMING SPACES.

On the interior, BNIM's design cleverly repurposed industrial remnants for new use or visual interest. The column-free North Engine Room contained a massive gantry crane and hook and a unique Texas Skylight, which were retained. The gantry crane and hook—formerly used to move heavy objects—found a new home in the Frost Studio as a visual element.

The South Boiler Room presented a number of very unique elements, including eight coal bunkers, two ash hoppers, conveyor system, and a chimney base that once supported an exterior smokestack removed in the 1970s. These elements were integrated, along with many others, into the new Bolender Center. The design team retrofitted the original coal funnels into pendant light fixtures, adapted the original coal bunkers to serve as dressing rooms, preserved a section of conveyor system that once transported ash and coal throughout the former power plant, and even adapted original pivot window hardware to support new light shelves. Also, to reference the placement of the Power House's original furnaces, BNIM integrated glass block infill to mark their former location in the new lobby space, allowing filtered daylight into the wardrobe workroom below.

Adding their own layer of history and reuse, KCB contributed numerous pipe fitting ballet barres that had moved with them from facility to facility over the years. The design team gave the barres permanent homes in the three largest studios including Frost Studio Theater. They were a perfect fit—industrial components in an industrial space now serving a new refined function.

09

SUSTAINABLE DESIGN

Sustainable design goals for the project were established very early in the design process. Redevelopment of an abandoned structure is inherently sustainable, adding density and community connectivity to an area. Thus, site selection alone helped the design team achieve many of the goals.

In the building's rehabilitation, the team integrated a new white roof, which reduces heat island effect, and added native site plantings in the former rail yard to minimize water use and help filter stormwater runoff. It reduced the building's energy consumption by installing efficient mechanical systems and took advantage of many of the materials already in the building, including the unique sloped steel elements of the bunkers to create functional spaces.

THE EXISTING WINDOW FRAMES, THOUGH APPROACHING 100 YEARS OLD, WERE IN REMARKABLY GOOD SHAPE, ALLOWING THE DESIGN TEAM TO REUSE THEM. NEW WINDOW SASHES WERE MADE WITH SUSTAINABLE FOREST ACCOYA WOOD IN COMBINATION WITH HIGH-PERFORMANCE GLAZING.

An efficient use of finish materials minimized resources and waste, along with low-emitting materials for the health and well-being of the occupants. Maximizing the use of daylight and views, which was offered by the huge expanses of existing windows, reduced artificial lighting use throughout the daytime and provided a connection to the outdoors for all. And, of course, the team configured the interior spaces to share and amplify natural daylight.

04 RESULTS

IGNITING BUSINESS GROWTH AND EVOLUTION

Through design, the Bolender Center beautifully embodies and supports the mission of the KCB's Company and School: to establish Kansas City Ballet as an indispensable asset of the community through exceptional performances, excellence in dance training and community education for all ages. Just as the building was carefully crafted to be a catalyst for growth and evolution, so was its name. The Todd Bolender Center for Dance & Creativity moniker not only honors one of the Ballet's most transformative leaders and identifies the building as a venue for dance, but in the word "Creativity," it also presents a positive challenge to KCB and a promise to the Kansas City community.

With nearly three times the square footage as that of KCB's previous facility, the Bolender Center allows a new density of activity. To a school looking to increase its student population, a professional company eager to grow, and a dance organization hoping to expand its range of studio classes to community members, the new capacity offers untapped potential.

The opening of the Bolender Center marked an influx of new talent, triggering an explosion in the number and types of creative offerings on KCB School's Studio Class schedule. Teachers and instructors came forth with dance and fitness options and, quite suddenly, KCB's studio schedule increased from four classes to thirteen including Boot Camp, Zumba®, Tap, Belly Dance, Yoga, Nia, Irish Step Dance, Flamenco, Jazz, Ballroom, Pilates, Hip Hop and Modern Dance. Enrollment in the studio classes quadrupled, from 187 in the 2010/2011 season to 535 in 2011/2012.

Similarly, the Ballet School experienced a significant increase in enrollment following the opening of the Bolender Center. In the 2011/2012 season, student enrollment—at the Bolender Center as well as the school's south campus in Johnson County, Kansas—climbed fifteen percent from the previous year.

But the new Bolender Center offers something more far-reaching as well.

Kansas City Ballet saw an increase of 70% in school enrollment from 2010 - 2011 the last year prior to the new buidling to this current year 2012 - 2013. Their ticket sales from 2010 - 11 season to 2011 - 12 season of their annual play Nutcracker rose by 28% and overall season attendance up by 92%.

2009/2010
527 STUDENTS

2010/2011
592 STUDENTS

2011/2012
1017 STUDENTS

STUDENT ENROLLMENT

Dancers performing during the opening activities of the Bolender Center on KC Dance Day

As a home for dance, the Bolender Center facility ranks among the best in the world. Ample, light-filled rehearsal spaces, an integrated theater, generously equipped locker rooms and showers, on-site physical therapy, and full access to Pilates apparatuses together provide accommodations that few other professional companies or schools can offer. For the professional company, this offers not only a world-class environment for creating and refining great artistic works, but it also presents an attractive recruitment tool for professional talent. Although KCB built a national reputation and sought-after company in its first fifty years, it had always lacked the accommodations and amenities needed to win out over other professional companies in the U.S.

Almost immediately after moving into the space, however, KCB saw a marked increase in the number of experienced professional dancers applying for company positions. With its light, space, design, studio sizes, amenities, urban location and relationship with the nearby performing arts center, the new Bolender Center offered something unique and desirable in the professional dance world: an inspiring place to work. In a professional sense, the Bolender Center has transformed KCB from a career starting point to a destination.

Indeed, the challenge of creativity is ever present in the minds of KCB leaders. Their vision is to grow—the school, the company and studio offerings—but, as importantly, they hope to cultivate talent, exploration, beauty, art and connection.

"AT A TIME WHEN MOST CITIES ARE REDUCING INVESTMENT IN THE ARTS, HOW REFRESHING IT IS TO BE IN KANSAS CITY WHERE THE ARTS ARE FLOURISHING."

Michael M. Kaiser
President, John F. Kennedy Center for the Performing Arts

SPARKING ECONOMIC VITALITY

Though the purpose of KCB has always been about enriching its community though the art of dance, KCB's space was never seen as a community asset. The Bolender Center changed that.

KCB's relocation to the Power House created a small ripple that continues to multiply and affect its community in profound and powerful ways. It has become a hub where artists and community find a synchronicity—a community venue, with dance as the fulcrum. It celebrates and disarms diversity, inviting citizens, businesses and art, in their many guises, to interact and create within the building.

For Kansas City residents, the Bolender Center is far more than just a place where dance is born and refined. Through the array of community classes, community members now use the building as a source of physical health and an outlet for creative expression. Parents of ballet students linger during class time, finding abundant and inviting areas to wait. Businesses host special events and other gatherings in the Bolender Center's voluminous lobby, Ellis Conference Room and Frost Studio Theater.

Local universities are also discovering great opportunities in the Bolender Center's studios and facilities. Students at the University of Missouri-Kansas City's Conservatory of Music and Dance, which shares a history of collaboration with KCB, are able to use the larger studios for showings or host performances in the Frost Studio.

For the cultural community, the new center provides an invaluable resource. KCB offers the 180-seat Michael and Ginger Frost studio to smaller dance and theater companies as a less formal performance space for their productions.

Also, for the first time in KCB's history, they have abundant studio and schedule capacity to accommodate and sustain new artistic growth programs, offering unprecedented opportunity to aspiring choreographers or artists looking to expand their artistic range.

Even tourism has benefitted from the Bolender Center's opening. The very act of restoring the historic Power House forever changed Kansas City history and created a new point of interest for tourists and history buffs. The restoration was the final piece needed to rehabilitate an area of Kansas City that is steeped in historic significance. Today, and for years to come, anyone visiting the area can tour the building and experience carefully preserved moments from an earlier time.

Perhaps the Bolender Center's most transformative effect, however, is evidenced by a physical culture shift taking place in Kansas City. The opening of the new home for KCB, in conjunction with that of the nearby Kauffman Center for the Performing Arts, created a powerful new mass in downtown Kansas City that is reorienting the city's arts community. Like a celestial body, this mass is attracting local and regional arts organizations and has spawned a civic movement to construct a cultural arts campus that will formally unite the Bolender Center, KCPA, the neighboring Crossroads Arts District and the Kansas City Conservatory of Music and Dance.

EVOKING BROAD APPEAL

Transforming the Power House was not easy. It was an intimidating proposal, a laborious and sometimes dangerous undertaking, and a complex funding challenge. But, in retrospect, it has proven a rewarding venture.

Since its grand opening in August 2011, the Todd Bolender Center for Dance & Creativity has gained an increasing community of supporters from all walks of life. The building embodies thoughtful design, respect for history, and a valuable contribution to its place—the products of deep commitment from each individual on the client, design and construction team.

In response, the Bolender Center has been embraced and celebrated by a variety of communities—civic, citizen, design and construction, cultural, and historical, among others. Its many awards include top honors from local and national design, trade and preservation organizations, civic organizations and mainstream news publications. Its success at national and international levels has continued to surprise and delight those whose efforts brought the vision to reality.

Indeed, this project, which began as a small spark of initiative to house a ballet company and school, has ignited a city and kindled a nation of supporters.

KANSAS CITY'S NOBLE POWER HOUSE HAS FOUND NEW PURPOSE AND A NEW SOURCE OF ENERGY THAT TRANSCENDS DANCE AND ART. THE EXTRAORDINARY TODD BOLENDER CENTER FOR DANCE & CREATIVITY EMBODIES THE POWER OF TRANSFORMATION.

—

ACCOLADES

2013	Architectural Record Good Design is Good Business Award
2013	Architizer A+ Award Finalist
2013	National AIA Institute Honor Award for Interior Architecture
2013	Preserve Missouri Award, Missouri Preservation
2012	AIA Kansas Honor Award
2012	National Preservation Honor Award, National Trust for Historic Preservation
2012	AIA Kansas City Honor Award
2012	Project of the Year, International Concrete Restoration Institute
2012	Sustainability Award, International Concrete Restoration Institute
2012	Best Renovation/Restoration Project, Award of Merit, ENR Midwest Best Projects
2012	Historic Renovation, KC Magazine Design Excellence Awards
2012	Capstone Award, Architectural Design, Kansas City Business Journal
2012	Cornerstone Award, Arts, Economic Development Corporation of Kansas City
2011	Excellence Award for Adaptive Reuse, Historic Kansas City Foundation
2011	Preservation Award, AIA Kansas City
2011	Project of the Year, International Concrete Repair Institute - Great Plains Chapter
2011	Award of Excellence, Historical Category, International Concrete Repair Institute - Great Plains Chapter

"THE BOLENDER CENTER IS ONE OF THE BEST DESIGNED AND THOUGHT-OUT DANCE FACILITIES IN THE COUNTRY, WHICH MEANS THAT IT IS ONE OF THE BEST IN THE WORLD."

William Whitener
Artistic Director, Kansas City Ballet

"EVERYTHING ABOUT THIS
RESTORATION—FROM THE
BUILDING'S USE, TO ITS DESIGN,
TO THE POWER OF BALLET,
THE POWER OF DANCE, THE
POWER OF ART—ALL OF THIS
RESTORES THAT ENERGY FOR
WHICH THE POWER HOUSE
WAS INITIALLY DESIGNED."

Cydney Millstein
Architectural & Historical Research, LLC

ENDNOTES

[1] William H. Wilson, *The City Beautiful Movement in Kansas City* (Columbia, Missouri: The University of Missouri, 1964), 104. Wilson points out that Hunt was "secretly commissioned" by the railroads as early as 1901. Besides Burnham, the other architectural firm in competition with Hunt was Howe, Hoit and Cutler, Kansas City.

[2] "The New Kansas City, MO. Union Passenger Station," *Railway Age Gazette* 57 (October 30, 1914), 799.

[3] Oehrlein & Associates, Architects and Robinson & Associates, "Historic Structures Report/Treatment Plan Kansas City Union Station." July 1, 1996, 2-14. The report also states that "A. H, Buckley was superintendent for the architect and "Hunt's full time, on-site representative during construction..." The location of Hunt's papers has not been found, if indeed they exist.

[4] It became critical to build a separate powerhouse that generated steam heat for buildings and cars instead of purchasing electrical service. See: "Power and Operating Section," *Electrical World* 65 (June 5, 1915), 1468.

[5] For an overview of power plant designs, see Allan Hubbard, "Power Provision and Steam Plant Design," *Architectural Forum* 39 (September 1923), 137-143.

[6] For those inclined toward industrial archeology, the following details of the equipment housed in the facility are provided: Among the original equipment stood two 1,250-kva, 2,300-volt 60-cycle turbo-generators, with exciters on the ends of shafts; three batteries of 1,016 h. p. high-reverse-setting Babcock & Wilcox boilers, two Nordberg cross-compound Corliss air compressors; one 60-ton and one 30-ton Carbondale exhaust system refrigerating plants for cooling drinking water and serving the needs of Union Station. An exhaust steam vacuum system heated the buildings within the complex, while live steam was fed to the locomotives at the roundhouse. See: *Railway Age Gazette* 57 (October 30, 1914), 803.

[7] Joan M. Brierton and Judith H. Robinson, "Kansas City Terminal Railway Company Kansas City Union Station Historic Resources Survey for Railyard Structures." June 1997, 12-19. And thanks to Kevin Amey, General Manager of the Kansas City Ballet, for his input.

[8] Donald Des Granges, "The Designing of Power Stations," *The Architectural Forum* 51 (September 1929), 371.

Scan the QR Code or go to **bnim.com/power**
to learn or share information about the adaptive reuse of historic buildings.

HISTORIC TAX CREDITS 101:
THE BASICS OF THE PROCESS

The following are general guidelines regarding the application process. It is important to note that in order to be eligible for the 20% federal tax credit the property must be listed in the National Register of Historic Places either individually or as a contributing resource to an historic district. Additionally, the property must be income producing and meet the minimum investment requirements.

01 Work with a preservation consultant and architect. These professionals should have an understanding and demonstrate a working knowledge of *The Secretary of the Interior's Standards*.

02 Submit two completed and signed copies of the Part II portion of the Historic Preservation Certification Application (and the Part I portion if the property is part of a district or not yet listed in the National Register) to the State Historic Preservation Office, along with clear photographs of the exterior and interior of the property, and proposed plans, for review.

03 After SHPO review, the application will be forwarded to the National Park Service for final review. Based on the anticipated cost of the project, a fee will be charged by the NPS for review.

04 Upon completion of the rehabilitation project, a Part III application is submitted to the SHPO and subsequently to the NPS for final certification.

05 Review time is 30 days at the state level and 45 days at the federal level.

06 If the state in which the property is located administers historic tax credits, the same rules for review apply.

There are several publications that are available through the internet that explain, in detail, the process of listing a building in the National Register of Historic Places, applying for historic tax credits and guidance on preserving, rehabilitating and restoring historic properties. A sampling of these publications includes:

nps.gov/nr/   nps.gov/tps/how-to-preserve/briefs.htm
nps.gov/tps/   nps.gov/tps/standards.htm

BNIM

With the support of our visionary clients, BNIM is redefining the national and global agenda for progressive planning strategies, responsible architecture and design excellence. We design creative environments that inspire behavior change and enhance the condition of people and the planet.

With 43 years of experience, BNIM has a reputation for thoughtful and responsive design, thorough technical competence and conscientious service. Throughout its history, the firm has focused on building healthy facilities through a balance of social, economic and environmental solutions. BNIM has emerged as a national leader in sustainability and innovative design while remaining committed to the regional community.

BNIM is known for its excellent technical capabilities enabling the successful execution of unique design challenges with remarkable and enduring results. The firm has a proven ability to effectively manage projects and schedules, rigorous quality control procedures and project costs throughout the life of our projects.

BNIM possesses not only the operational precision, but also the design sensitivity and architectural sophistication essential to envision complex projects. We are proud of our reputation for precision and our documented record of adherence to schedule and budget. We have demonstrated that this kind of operational excellence can, and indeed should, be linked to an appreciation of the aesthetic and spiritual qualities of a place.

Steve McDowell, FAIA, is Director of Design for BNIM, the recipient of the 2011 AIA Firm Award. As an innovator, his workplace is a laboratory for exploring ideas related to site, environment and technical investigation. He believes in a lively exchange of thoughts to stimulate exploration and sustain innovation. Steve maintains that good design is about people – their health, productivity and lifting the human spirit through design. His work is setting new standards in high performance design in projects across the country. His previous book, *FLOW*, chronicles the making of the first Living Building, The Omega Center for Sustainable Living in Rhinebeck, NY.

Michael M. Kaiser is President of the John F. Kennedy Center for the Performing Arts. He has expanded the educational and artistic programming for the nation's center for the performing arts and has overseen a major renovation effort of most of the Center's theaters. As Kennedy Center President, Mr. Kaiser is responsible for the artistic and financial health of the Center's extensive theater, jazz, chamber music, and dance seasons as well as its affiliates the National Symphony Orchestra VSA, and Washington National Opera.

Marlon Blackwell, FAIA, is a practicing architect in Fayetteville, Arkansas, and serves as Distinguished Professor and Department Head in the Fay Jones School of Architecture at the University of Arkansas. Working outside the architectural mainstream, his architecture is based in design strategies that draw upon vernaculars and the contradictions of place; strategies that seek to transgress conventional boundaries for architecture. Work produced in his professional office, Marlon Blackwell Architect, has received national and international recognition with numerous design awards and significant publication in books, architectural journals and magazines. Blackwell received the 2012 Architecture Prize from the American Academy of Arts and Letters. A monograph of his early work, "An Architecture of the Ozarks: The Works of Marlon Blackwell," was published by Princeton Architectural Press in 2005. He was selected by The International Design Magazine, in 2006, as one of the ID Forty: Undersung Heroes. He received his undergraduate degree from Auburn University (1980) and a M. Arch II degree from Syracuse University in Florence, Italy (1991).

David Buege is Professor and Fay Jones Chair in Architecture at the University of Arkansas, and former director of the Architecture Program. He has taught at Auburn University, Mississippi State University and the New Jersey Institute of Technology. He was interim director of Auburn's Rural Studio for a year. He received his B.S. in Environmental Design from the University of Wisconsin-Milwaukee, studied for one year at the Institute for Architecture and Urban Studies in New York, and received his M.Arch. from Princeton University. He has worked in the offices of Eisenman Architects and Bartos-Rhodes Architects in New York.

John G. Waite, FAIA, has over forty-five years' experience in the restoration, rehabilitation, and adaptive-use of existing buildings, as well as the design of new structures in historic contexts. He is a fellow of the American Institute of Architects and received a National AIA Design Award for the restoration of the Baltimore Cathedral. His firm's projects include dozens of historic churches, five state capitols,; Mt. Vernon, Lincoln Memorial, Statue of Liberty, Tweed Courthouse, and Blair House, the President's Guest House. Current projects include Sagamore Hill, Ralph Adams Cram's, Church of All Saints' Ashmont, Yale University School of Music complex at Norfolk, Connecticut, and Thomas Jefferson's Rotunda at the University of Virginia. He has written more than fifty books and articles and has taught at Columbia and Cornell Universities.

Cydney Millstein is an architectural historian and founder of Architectural & Historical Research, LLC, in Kansas City, Missouri, with nationwide experience in the field for 30 years. Her work includes the examination and documentation of buildings and industrial typologies for a variety of clients, both public and private. Ms. Millstein's honors include the two National Trust for Historic Preservation Honor Awards, the Osmond Overby Award, and the U.S. GSA Design Award. Her book, Houses of Missouri: 1870-1940, co-authored with Dr. Carol Grove, was published by Acanthus Press, NY, in October 2008. She is currently working with Dr. Grove on a book about the landscape architecture firm of Hare and Hare to be published by the Library of American Landscape History in 2014.

Credits

Many thanks to all those that have made this project possible, including those noted below as well as donors, patrons and friends of the Kansas City Ballet.

Contributors

Jeffrey J. Bentley, Executive Director, Kansas City Ballet
William Whitener, Artistic Director, Kansas City Ballet
Rick Schladweiler, Project Architect, BNIM
Rich McGuire, Principal Engineer, Structural Engineering Associates
J.E. Dunn Construction

Project Team

Owner Power House Properties
Tenant Kansas City Ballet
General Manager of KCB Kevin Amey
Architect BNIM
Owner's Representative MC Realty Group
General Contractor J.E. Dunn Construction
Design-Build MEP Contractors Gibbens Drake Scott, Inc, Mark One Electric Company, Inc., & US Engineering, and National Fire Suppression
Structural Engineer Structural Engineering Associates, Inc.
Civil Engineer Taliaferro and Browne
Landscape Architect BNIM
Acoustical Engineer Acoustical Design Group, Inc.
Code Consulting FSC Inc.
Hardware Consulting Studio 08 Consultants
KC Ballet Consultants
Preservation Consultant Architectural & Historical Research, LLC
Theatre Consultant Harvest Productions Inc.
Exhibit Design Eisterhold Associates Inc.
Exhibit Fabricator Exhibit Associates
Furniture, Fixtures and Equipment Contract Furnishings

Author

Stephen McDowell
Foreword by Michael M. Kaiser
Introduction by Marlon Blackwell
Essay by John G. Waite
Essay by Cydney Millstein

Book Design

BNIM
Designer Beena Ramaswami
Writer Keri Maginn
Project Coordinator Erin Gehle

Imagery

Farshid Assassi, Assassi Productions *pages 6, 29, 37, 46, 58-59, 73, 76-77, 82, 83, 86, 88, 89, 99, 101* | Mike Sinclair *pages 2-3, 11, 70-71, 72, 78-79, 92, 112-113* | Dan Videtich *front & back cover, pages 31, 88, 106, 111* | Cody Lovetere *pages 31, 46, 47* | Richard Welnowski *pages 31, 33, 88, 96* | Kansas City Ballet *pages 103, 105* | Leonard Fohn *page 38-39, 54, 56-57, 74-75, 85, 91, 95* | Missouri Valley Room, Special Collections, Kansas City Public Library, Kansas City, Missouri *pages 13, 14-15, 16, 18-19, 22-23* | Power House Historic Photos *pages 24, 26, 27 Electrical World, Vol. 65, No. 23* | P-Tn/Eric Berndt *pages 20-21, 31* | BNIM *All others*

Published by

ORO Editions
Publishers of Architecture, Art, and Design
Gordon Goff: Publisher
Usana Shadday: Production Manager
www.oroeditions.com | info@oroeditions.com

Color Separations and Printing

ORO Group Ltd.
Printed in China.

Copyright © 2013 by ORO Editions
ISBN: 978-1-941806-15-9
10 09 08 07 06 5 4 3 2 1 First Edition

This book was printed and bound using a variety of sustainable manufacturing processes and materials including soy-based inks, acqueous-based varnish, VOC- and formaldehyde-free glues, and phthalate-free laminations. The text is printed using offset sheetfed lithographic printing process in four color on 157gsm premium matte art paper with an off-line gloss acqueous spot varnish applied to all photographs.

ORO Editions makes a continuous effort to minimize the overall carbon footprint of its publications. As part of this goal, ORO Editions, in association with Global ReLeaf, arranges to plant trees to replace those used in the manufacturing of the paper produced for its books. Global ReLeaf is an international campaign run by American Forests, one of the world's oldest nonprofit conservation organizations. Global ReLeaf is American Forests' education and action program that helps individuals, organizations, agencies, and corporations improve the local and global environment by planting and caring for trees.

Library of Congress data: Available upon request

For information on our distribution, please visit our website: www.oroeditions.com